Who We Are

Seven Christian Identities to Shape Your Life

Who We Are

Seven Christian Identities
to Shape Your Life

JAKE DOBERENZ

McGahan

MCGAHAN PUBLISHING HOUSE

www.mphbooks.com

Requests for information should be sent to:

info@mphbooks.com

Cover Design by Andrew Waters

ISBN 978-1-951252-10-6

contents

"Jesus came to announce to us that an identity based on success, popularity and power is a false identity – an illusion! Loudly and clearly he says: 'You are not what the world makes you; but you are children of God.'"

Henri J.M. Nouwen

the starting point

SOMETIMES you are watching a show and you see an actor who you recognize appear on screen. Unless you are a film buff like my brother, most of us can't recall the names of most actors and actresses that pop up on the screen. But our brains immediately try to place this person in the grand scheme of things. Often, we recognize them by their work or a previous character. For instance, when Daniel Radcliffe is in a movie, we almost instinctively say, "Hey, it's Harry Potter!" Many actors get famous for one role or for playing one kind of character—that's just how Hollywood works sometimes. As viewers, we get used to seeing people in certain ways. Watching an actor go from comedy to drama can be cringy because we just aren't used to it. Or sometimes watching "Disney princesses" grow up into sexualized, tough girl characters can be jarring at first (Like Anne Hathaway, who went from sweet, awkward girl to a sophisticated elite assassin type). There's also this funny thing that happens where one generation associates certain actors with certain roles differently than another: Millennials know Sean Astin as Samwise from *Lord of the Rings,* but Gen Z knows him as Bob from *Stranger Things.*

For so many of these actors, their identity is wrapped up in the kinds of roles they often play or the key roles which made them famous. They are who the world knows them best for playing. This is just one example of how our brain takes a shortcut and boxes a person in—so now, for our convenience, Jennifer Anniston *is* Rachel from *Friends.* While most of us haven't reached a level of fame where people will say, "Hey, you're that girl who XYZ," many people have some distinctive qualities whether we like to admit it or not. Either others cast these stereotypes on us, or we choose to think of ourselves in these terms. Maybe we like this identity, or maybe we don't. Like it or not, we have an identity.

the triangle of identity

"WHO AM I?" is a question that all of us ask ourselves at some point. When we begin the transition to legal adults and are expected to pull our weight in society, questions about our identity and purpose in life bubble to the surface. When life goes sideways and we have to reconsider our place in the world, pursuing (either a new or old) identity becomes a survival mechanism. In these situations, we ask: What defines me? What makes me *me?* Whether we verbally ask these questions or not, a struggle for identity, belonging, and a sense of self is especially prevalent in the young adult years.

I know identity means different things to different people. In many ways, it's a catch-all term that tries to lump a lot of different elements into it. Despite the messiness of the term, it seems to me it is safe to say each person has a core of what makes them different. Every "I" is the sum of a body, mind, personality, actions, etc. For my undergraduate Bible degree, I took the class Counseling for Ministers, and the professor introduced us to a triangle made of three sides: thinking, feeling, and behaving. In counseling, if you want to change a person's feelings, you might tackle it from the angles of fixing the thinking and behaving. But for our present purposes, the triangle does a good job of describing all that makes us up. If the corners are our THOUGHTS, ACTIONS, and EMOTIONS, then the whole triangle can be labeled IDENTITY. It is the sum of ourselves.

Yet, this isn't the full picture. It can't be—it assumes our identity is trapped only inside of us. While America might prioritize individualism, in other countries and in much of the ancient world, your identity isn't in your one-of-a-kind personality, but in your group. Your family, tribe, city, or class level determines who you are and what you do in life. Thus, to be more accurate and fair, we can say that the triangle of identity is also found in a larger sea of identities. Whether we like it or not, our thoughts, actions, and emotions are often influenced by forces beyond ourselves like groups, religious beliefs, societal expectations, and, of course, sin. So if we wish to have some control over our identity, we can't just change ourselves. We have to change what we put into ourselves.

issues with identity

The West glorifies identity. In America, we often celebrate our differences and those things that make us special and unique. We get specific certifications, join niche Facebook groups, or express ourselves visually and verbally in a variety of ways. If someone were to tell us we *can't* express a certain part of our inner core, it can feel like a personal assault. It hurts deep. It's dehumanizing. Our immediate reaction is often to fight back, to protect our identity at all costs. We often build our lives on our perceived self-identity, so if that identity foundation is torn down, we are left completely aimless. In the West, we proudly embrace the platitude "to thine own self be true." Let's not forget, though, that this phrase is from *Hamlet*, not the Bible.

Certainly, it is a major problem that so much energy is spent on individual expression. It's easy to point out the flaws in the system, call someone a "snowflake," and then cast off the whole modern quest for identity. There are plenty of examples of identities that seem destructive or negative or weird—there could be a temptation to tell someone to just stop being "weird" and act "normal." Identity seems a fruitless liberal cause. However, I have two main reasons, however, to defend this so-called identity quest.

Firstly, let's just accept that the world we live in requires us to think about ourselves. Advertisements, movies, books, music, self-help gurus—everyone is asking us to be "who we really are." But it's not like the modern era has invented identity since people for eons have had to think about themselves in order to establish governments, religions, communities, and art. Even refusing to acknowledge your identity is just surrendering to the cultural identity that flows around you. At some point in our lives, we must ask and answer the question: "Who am I?" It is an unavoidable question.

Secondly, the quest is important because the Bible spends so much time on identity formation, even if we miss it. The Bible also asks us to be "who we really are," but the question means something way different than how culture today uses it. We must be *something* since we can't be *nothing*, and Scripture constantly urges us not to let the world or sinful flesh determine the *something* that we become. In fact, our status as those who are "made in the image of God" (Gen. 1:26-27) forces us to wrestle with our identity as image-bearers. Theologian Joe Jones understands that our image-bearing status has a lot to say about our destinies. Jones says that God summons us "into a future destiny of life with God and with other humans and with the whole creation." He continues, "Being so created, human spirits are launched on a great adventure in which they are called to become—to fully enact—their potential endowment."[i] Humans are always incomplete without Christ. Only in Christ do we found our proper identity. To be a Christian is to work out our identity on God's terms and discover what that means for how we live our life. It's our duty to ask these pivotal questions about our identity while being sure our answers are shaped by our Christian convictions.

In one sense, identities cannot be "wrong." Some identities are simply preferences (like a Trekkie vs. a Star Wars fan). Identities are not concrete "things" and so exist in a neutral space. However, a person can measure the goodness of an identity. We can look at its behavioral fruits, in how you live out your identity. We can examine the foundations, as we can (and often do) build up identities on false expectations, worldviews, beliefs, or feelings. Or we can measure the effects of the identity on ourselves—does it destroy or give life? Sometimes identities might be built on good things for all the wrong reasons, which can also screw up the created identity. Undoubtedly, we can go wrong when all the pressure to create an identity is laid on fallible people, like yourself, your society, and the fallen world. As Christians, we know sin is a reality. Humans are prone to believe false things, to feel things they should not, and to get themselves in sticky situations. The world is a mess, and that means even our desires and our own picture of truth might be off. As identities compete for our allegiance, some are certainly better than others.

This present work mentions seven false identities that commonly claim our lives. Certainly, there are more negative identities that compete for our time, attention, and loyalty. I chose the seven because I believe they most clearly battle for the souls of young adult Christians in our current culture. These seven false identities are not necessarily anti-Christian. None of them count as "sin" per se except for the first identity, which is actually an *identity in sin* itself! Most of these are just desires out of proportion. False or unconstructive identities are filling a type of longing or desire within us that prevents the Spirit from fully being at work in our lives. Nevertheless, Satan would be happy for you to embrace one of these earthly identities.

Each of the seven false identities is met with a positive identity to replace it. When we throw off the identities of the world, we must replace them with *something*. Getting rid of bad isn't enough; good must take its place. Those of faith need to find a solid foundation on which to build a new identity, an identity rooted in Christ, that more accurately meets those underlying longings. I hope not just to tear down distracting identities but to present a positive way forward. These new identities meet our innermost desires, address the problems we face as human creatures, and point toward something better that God has prepared for us. Each positive identity flows from the way Jesus lived and died; each identity is a facet of Christ's identity. As explained below, Christian practice finds Christ as our true north and as our endgame.

the source of our identity

In our struggle to create a new identity and put off the old, we must first understand the source of our new identity and how this identity is not like anything else.

Christians should get our identity from Christ—it's right in the name, in fact. God, through Christ, has established us as a special people. We are "a chosen race, a royal priesthood, a holy nation, a people for [God's] own possession," 1 Peter 2:9 says. Becoming a Christian is getting an extreme makeover, becoming a whole new person. The lifestyle change in following Christ cannot be understated. There is no 9 to 5 with the faith. Christianity requires a complete change in identity, but the change is far more significant than switching from a goth kid to a nerd. Paul writes in Galatians 2:20 that "I have been crucified with Christ. It is no longer I who live, but Christ who lives in me. And the life I now live in the flesh I live by faith in the Son of God, who loved me and gave himself for me." This transformation into a "new life" encompasses all human experiences—thoughts, feelings, behavior, and social relations. The Christian walk looks like this: we move out, Christ moves in. Our identity is now in Christ.

The goal of transformation is to be shaped into Christ and by Christ, a process that Scot McKnight insightfully calls "Christoformity" to describe the way conformed to Christ in Christ's life, death, and resurrection.[ii] The New

Testament is clear many times that to be like Christ is to have the qualities of Christ in us. However, this idea is not just a simple question of "What Would Jesus Do?" Christ provides more than an example for living, but he is the agent and essence of our transformation. Grant Macaskill, in a helpful work called *Living in Union with Christ*, notes that "we can never talk about the moral activity of a Christian without always, in the same breath, talking about Jesus, because the goal of our salvation is not that we become morally better versions of ourselves but that we come to inhabit and to manifest *his* moral identity."[iii] Our task is thus to embrace the identity bestowed upon us rather than to build one from within ourselves.

Christoformity is especially evident throughout the letter to the Philippians. In the opening of the letter, Paul expresses his desire that the Philippians live their life "in a manner worthy of the gospel of Christ" (1:27). In Philippians 2, specific behavior—selflessness and humility—are directly connected to the example of Christ. Paul introduces a hymn about Jesus' humility in coming down to earth (2:6-11) with "Let the same mind be in you that was in Christ Jesus" (2:5). In chapter 3, Paul explains that even though he has reason to boast in human terms, he considers all that useless because he desires to "know" Christ above all (3:8). In 3:10, Paul is more specific in his desire to be transformed into Christ, announcing he wants to become "like him in his death." Paul also assures his readers that Christ "will transform the body of our humiliation that it may be conformed to the body of his glory" (3:21). Philippians demonstrates time and time again that our thoughts and actions—our very identity—all should stem from our connection with Jesus Christ.

There is no perfect metaphor to describe what it means to embrace a Christ-centered identity. Paul bounces between several metaphors like "putting on Christ" (Gal. 3:27), and he often plays around with the vaguer idea of being "transformed" (Rom. 8:28-29, 12:1-2; Gal. 2:19-20; 4:19; 2 Cor. 3:18; 5:17; Eph. 4:22-24). One of his most powerful descriptors of all this is a phrase we do not even recognize as a metaphor: "in Christ" (Rom. 6:11, 23; 8:1-2; 12:5; 1 Cor. 1:30; 3:1; 4:10). Especially in the early chapters of 1st Corinthians, Paul is really concerned with his audience being "in Christ" rather than locating themselves under any other authority. Though some Scripture talks about Christ being

13

inside us, Scripture also demands that we get *inside Christ*. New Testament scholar Michael Gorman calls this a life of *mutual indwelling* or *reciprocal residence*.[iv] This is the spirit of what Jesus says throughout John 15. "Abide in me, and I in you" (v.4), Jesus tells his faithful followers.

In seeking Christoformity in our lives, it requires us to properly locate our identities. Rowan Williams, former Archbishop of Canterbury in the Church of England, understands our goal as Christians as to get "located" properly. He exclaims in an address to the World Council of Churches,

And it can be put most forcefully, even shockingly, if we say that Christians identify themselves not only as servants of the anointed king but as Christ. Their place in the world is his place. By allowing themselves to be caught up in his witness and doing what his authority makes possible for them, in work and worship, they stand where he stands. The Christian Scriptures say that believers bear the name of Christ, that this name is written on their foreheads, that their life together is a material 'body' for the anointed king on earth. Christian identity is to belong in a place that Jesus defines for us. By living in that place, we come to some degree to share his identity, to bear his name, and to be in the same relationships he has with God and with the world.[v]

As we commence on our identity expedition, discovering identities that Christians should embrace as well as should not embrace, we have to keep Jesus at the center of the quest. While we will pull examples of good and bad identities from all over Scripture, Christ is still the ultimate good example. After all, Jesus lived as wholly human and wholly God. He knows what it's like to have two "natures." Similarly, through a relationship with Christ, empowered by the Holy Spirit, we are adopting the imprint of God on our human souls as we seek to live out the Gospel more fully. Conforming to Christ changes not just how we see ourselves, but actually, on the deepest levels, *who we are*.

We can't expect spiritual formation to happen overnight—this is a long process. But this book attempts to help a Christian through this awkward process. Identify formation—or rather, reformation—is not an easy process, or everyone would be doing it all the time! I do advise that no one goes on this journey alone. The title of the work is *Who We Are* and not *Who You Are* because the entire Christian community is together working on putting away the old and being a new creation. Finding those that have gone before who now faithfully live in Christ is highly recommended. I urge you, dear reader, do not embark on this journey alone. This book is just the beginning. I hope to help chip away negative identities and point you to Christ and his incredible vision for your life. This process is a lifetime of work.

"Grace does not abolish nature,
but completes it."
Thomas Aquinas

chapter one

Sin / God's Grace

C HURCH camp was always an emotional turmoil for me. It was great for my faith, terrible for my social anxiety. When I entered the older kid camps, silliness decreased, and things got a bit more serious. In one particular weekend fall camp, each youth group wandered off to a spot in the woods to reflects on the events of the weekend. As darkness fell in that wood covering in the forest, somehow, things turned serious. I mean, *really* serious. We started confessing our sins out loud to one another, in the presence of guys and girls. The typical joker types turned somber. The quiet ones spoke up. In the complete darkness, we confessed our deepest struggles. Particularly, I remember many boys confessing an addiction to pornography. That kind of rawness didn't even happen when it was just guys, but this was guys *and* girls. Something about the moment made everyone come clean.

There wasn't a dry eye anywhere.

I don't really remember what all was said. I can't even recall if I said anything. What does stick with me is everyone's reaction. When teens bore their souls and admitted their darkest sins, they were met with forgiveness, support, and plenty of grace. I can't comment on people's inner thoughts, but it was one of the closest moments our youth group ever experienced. And it started with everyone recognizing their problems, issues, and most serious sins.

Sin is a part of our lives. All of us have messed up. Some would say it is what makes us human. If you claim you've never sinned, well, you're lying—which is a sin! It's not hard to see the world is broken, people are messed up, and this isn't Heaven. The imperfections on this earth are quite visible in those around us but also in ourselves. While churches often preach about the reality of sin, some stress our sinful nature much more than others. In some movements, sin is what *defines* us.

But there is a better way. There is a truer identity. Us being "sinners" is not the end of the story.

defining sin

Though "sin" is talked about quite a bit in churches, it's one of those religious words that gets thrown around but never really *defined*. That is probably because it's a tall order. Occasionally, we use "sin" as synonymous with anything that is a bad idea—yet, that doesn't seem to capture the full meaning of "sin." While we might agree the act of smoking is a bad idea for your health, it's not really something most people would call a "sin." If I j-walk across the street, this act is illegal, but does it really reach the great grand category of Sin?

The Bible uses lots of different terms for sin: trespass, transgress, iniquity, evil, or wickedness. The classical way of describing sin—the way I heard a few times growing up in the church—is that sin means "missing the mark." This is not a terrible definition, but I find that the definition, well, "misses the mark." It does not fully capture what sin means. So what is sin? The present project does not have the space to guide the dear reader through the maze of scholarship trying to precisely pin down sin. Nor what I expect many to be interested in the academic debates over the subject. However, there are a few quick detours we need to make before we talk any more about sin and especially how sin affects our identities.

There are a lot of definitions. One idea about sin takes it in a genetic sense—sin is a disease. The concept of "original sin" comes largely from Augustine, who sees Adam and Eve's disobedience toward God as affecting all humankind thereafter. This is one reason some traditions baptize infants since even infants are born with the "disease" of sin. A second definition of sin makes sin out to be a legal term: the Bible's "thou shalts" and the "thou shalt nots" guide you on what is good and what is not. If you break a rule, you get a well-deserved punishment. A third way to understand sin is to imagine sin as a "cosmic force." Sin is personified as an evil being, perhaps synonymous with Satan; it's the devil on your shoulder that tempts you, it's trying to control you, and it will stop at nothing to manipulate you into turning from God. A fourth view takes sin as a social construct or built into unjust structures of oppression in society. Often associated with liberation theology, this view sees sin, not as a disease, legal term, or force, but as a result of poorly constructed societies that cause hurt and negativity toward others.

As a way forward, knowing that I will not settle the debate once and for all, I would like to offer a definition that plays on all four of these views. The Book of Romans (especially chapters 5-8, where the noun sin appears 42 times) serves as a case study because it depicts sin in several different ways. In 5:12-21, it appears that sin is like a genetic disease that is passed down from Adam. But chapter 6 makes it sound like sin is a choice. Paul emphatically writes: "Let not sin therefore reign in your mortal body, to make you obey its passions. Do not present your members to sin as instruments for unrighteousness" (6:12-13b). Then chapter seven speaks of sin as if it is almost synonymous with the law (probably the Torah, the law of the Hebrew people). Romans 7:7 explicitly says: "if it had not been for the law, I would not have known sin." In the midst of chapter 7, however, sin is made out almost like a cosmic force. Paul writes: "For I do not understand my own actions. For I do not do what I want, but I do the very thing I hate. …So now it is no longer I who do it, but sin that dwells within me." (7:15, 17).

So Paul isn't much help in clearing this up!

From the beginning of the letter, Paul paints a pretty depressing picture of the world and its relationship with sin. In chapter 1, verse 18 starts with the strong statement, "For the wrath of God is revealed from heaven against all ungodliness and unrighteousness of men, who by their unrighteousness suppress the truth." From there, Paul continues describing the wicked state of the world with a whopping 41 designations and examples of sin!

Then you turn to Romans 2. Paul flips the script. A New Testament professor of mine once called this "the greatest literary Judo move of all time." After describing how wicked the pagan world is, Paul then says, "Therefore you have no excuse, O man, every one of you who judges. For in passing judgment on another, you condemn yourself because **you, the judge, practice the very same things**." In other words: you guys are just as bad. He continues this rhetorical move in 3:9, where he affirms "both Jews and Greeks, are under sin"—that is, the power of sin. In the next two verses, he quotes: "None is righteous, no, not one; no one understands; no one seeks for God." As Romans 3:23 makes plainly clear: "all have sinned and fall short of the glory of God." Summarizing the power of sin in Romans, New Testament scholar Beverly Gaventa writes: "Sin cannot be avoided or passed over, it can only be either served or defeated."[vi]

We know that even as baptized believers, we mess up. Constantly. We commit sins that are supposed to categorize the pagans—the group Paul is writing about in Romans 1. Sometimes we look just like those on the "outside." We sympathize with Paul when he says: "For I do not do what I want, but I do the very thing I hate" (7:15). It's clear that, yeah, humans are messed up—even the Christians. We aren't that great. For most people, doing good isn't second nature. It takes work. It takes practice. It takes divine intervention. Sin, unfortunately, categorizes the human state.

Since Paul does not clear up the definition of sin, I won't either. Instead, let's assume that sin is multi-dimensional. It works within us and within society as a whole. As Gary Anderson points out, the difficulty in pinning down sin is that writers throughout history have attempted to capture the concept with metaphors, but as time moves forward, new metaphors and systems of thinking arise.[vii] D.A. Carson makes another great point: "One simply cannot make sense of the Bible without a profound and growing sensitivity to the multifaceted and powerful ways the Bible portrays sin."[viii] Sin is complex and abstract, almost as if the concept itself is a purposefully alluding definition. Perhaps that is the case—after all, this force is above and beyond us, so why do we pretend as our human minds could ever really grasp it?

how sin shows up as identity

An extreme focus on sin is not always healthy, even if it is true that sin is a significant part of who we are. Life isn't just defined by those that do "bad stuff" and those that do "good stuff"—there are more important distinctions in life. While we by no means should *shrug off* our sinful nature or ignore the cosmic powers of Sin that continue to attack us even as followers of Christ, we do not have our identity in sin.

Though it is difficult to define sin concretely, that doesn't stop well-meaning Christians from defining our identity in terms of sin. There are several ways this overreliance on sin might manifest in the world today. Many of these are likely Christians *trying* to live faithfully. They see the reality of sin in scripture and our own lives, so they stress it. I want to make clear that focusing on sin *is not* a sin, yet that doesn't

21

stop some of the policing methods that go along with this overreliance from being harmful to people. It's a misguided overemphasis—sin does not really define who we are.

Many churches want us to remember we are sinful people. There are a wide variety of go-too passages, many that list sins ranging from murder to lying, that are used to scare people into being obedient to God. Involved in what's nicknamed "fire and brimstone," preaching is often implicitly teaching a theology that roots our identity in sin—and then slaps us in the face and tells us to change! Through these teachers, we are reminded that Jeremiah 17:9 says, "The heart is deceitful above all things, and desperately sick; who can understand it?" And that Paul recognizes that even in himself, there is a pull toward sin (Rom. 7:15). We might call these folks "fundamentalist" preachers, those churches with strict rules that stress judgment for sins at the pulpit every Sunday. Admittedly, a little guilt can be helpful. But I fear the over-emphasis on sin from the pulpit is likely to craft people who are seeing themselves as Sinners and not as the Saved. If God becomes the "cosmic cop" and not a redeemer, loving father, and life-giver, then the whole focus of faith shifts the wrong way from what God intended.

The metanarrative of Scripture is often divided between Pre-Fall (Genesis 3) and Post-Fall (everything after Genesis 3). This narrative model correctly points out that sin affects us, affects creation, affects the structure of everything. Undoubtedly, we are in a Post-Fall world, one where sin runs rampant. But we shouldn't minimize both the role of Jesus and the role of our new identity in Christ as another major part of the narrative. The image of God, the *imago deo*, in Genesis 1 still remains with us even though it's corrupted. Theologian Marc Cortez reminds us that though sin is the reality now, it is not our true state. "Everything about human persons and human existence since the fall stands under the pervasive influence of sin. Any adequate anthropology must address the fact that real humanity as we actually see and experience it is corrupted by sin." However, Cortez continues,

Consequently, we cannot arrive at an understanding of true humanity—humanity as God intended it to be and which God is restoring in and through the person of Jesus Christ—through empirical observations of humanity as it actually is. Once again, then, we are led back to the person and work of Jesus Christ, the righteous one, as the one adequate starting point of a valid theological anthropology.[ix]

It might seem pious to stress our "wretched state." But Jesus changes everything. Jesus overcomes the power of sin. Especially as changed believers, our reality must be interpreted through what Jesus did and not what Satan did. The opposite of preaching a sin-heavy sermon is actually not to preach a love-heavy sermon. Sometimes, more progressive preachers are accused of focusing on love all the time and never on sin. That's not a terrible critique. The opposite of a sin-heavy sermon is not a love-heavy sermon but a grace-heavy sermon.

So-called "Purity Culture" is another great example. This movement of the 1990s and early 2000s (though it still exists in many contexts today) often focuses on the overwhelming desires of the flesh and so puts serious boundaries in place to prevent sexual promiscuity (such as no kissing, chaperones on dates, etc.). I read Joshua Harris' *I Kissed Dating Goodbye* in high school and was quite convicted by it. I remember a description—a dream, I think—of a woman getting married to a man but being "chained" to all the men she had previously slept with. It's not hard to see how the purity movement puts someone's identity in sin. The danger of this movement, for many people but especially women, is its labeling of non-virgins as "damaged goods." As if grace does not exist. It additionally assumes that *purity* is about making good choices when actually, purity comes from God alone.

There is also a well-meaning narrative about the compounding effects of sin. Randy Alcorn, in the opening pages of his book *The Purity Principle*, falls into this trap with the examples he gives of risky sexual behavior. He tells the story of one guy who committed adultery, then later ended up in prison for molesting his daughter. He tells the story of a young teen who had sex with her boyfriend—next thing you know, she's sleeping around left and right and gets an abortion—then she turns to drugs, prostitution, more abortions, and was raped. That girl's boyfriend apparently had lost interest in spiritual things and feels "empty." Alcorn paints a grim picture of anyone who's had sex outside of marriage—it spirals out of control, your sin eats you up and defines who you are. Certainly, Alcorn admits that these sins can be forgiven, but he is drastically overemphasizing the effects of sin on our spiritual state. He quotes Jonah 2:8, "Those who cling to worthless idols forfeit the grace that could be theirs" (NIV). They (rightly) calls sex an idol.[x] Yet, I can't help but sit uncomfortably with this idea that someone "forfeits" grace because of their mistakes—what a grim (and incorrect) view of reality.

For all believers, our identity is not in the powers of Sin. It is in God's gift of grace. This is a beautiful thing; it's freeing. Being defined by sin traps us; it gives us a fear-based relationship with God. Yet grace changes everything. Jesus righted the wrongs of the world and forgave sins past, present, and future. I'm thankful for Jesus because it means I am more than my sin.

we are under God's grace

All this demands a question of us: If sin is so pervious and powerful, isn't it naturally incorporated in our identity?

While sin is powerful, it is thrown off when we move into an identity in grace. Paul makes this move in Romans. Ironically, grace shows

24

up in the same sentence as the oft-quoted "for all have sinned." Paul writes in Romans 2:32-26:

> for all have sinned and fall short of the glory of God, and are justified by his grace as a gift, through the redemption that is in Christ Jesus, whom God put forward as a propitiation by his blood, to be received by faith. This was to show God's righteousness, because in his divine forbearance he had passed over former sins. It was to show his righteousness at the present time, so that he might be just and the justifier of the one who has faith in Jesus.

This Romans 3 passage is filled with some fancy and churchy terminology that can make it difficult to understand. First, let's tackle what it means to be justified. Justification is a fancy theological term referring to our status before God. In simple terms, it means that even though we have sin, we are "counted" as being righteous. While the rules of the cosmos say that our guilt earns us condemnation, God, being the Judge, lets those with faith off the hook. Our response is to glorify the Lord and to avoid sin, and work in the Kingdom of God on earth. The best example of justification is what is said in Genesis 15:6 when Abraham's belief in God was "counted to him as righteousness."

What about grace? Romans 3 says we are justified *by grace*. Here's the thing, grace is a loaded term in the Greek language, and so translating it effectively into our language is difficult. It literally means "favor" or "gift." Because Greek has fewer words than English, it's used in a lot of ways. It can refer to the gift of a wealthy person to a poorer person, and it can refer to the honor or praise that the receiver of the gift gives their benefactor. In this case, the "grace" is what God gives us. And by definition, grace given by a benefactor or a patron is undeserved. The poorer person can never pay it back in a financial sense; they can only relay praise and honor. Ephesians 2:8 says, "For by grace you have been saved through faith. And this is not your own doing; it is the gift of God."

Sometimes, though, God gives wrath when God's gift of grace is not appreciated. We can better understand Romans 1 when we see the wrath as a response to an ungrateful world. Luckily though, we ungrateful people—sinners—have been presented a solution: Jesus. While technically our status as sinners puts a divide between God and us, with Christ, this is no longer the case. David deSilva, a New Testament scholar, writes in his book about the social world of the New Testament that "God shows the supreme, fullest generosity (not just what God has to spare!) toward those who are God's enemies (not just ingrates, but those who have been actively hostile to God and God's desires)."[xi] God's love changes everything.

We get the same idea present in Romans 3 in Ephesians 2:1-10, though this one is longer and more descriptive. Ephesians 2 also mentions the reality of Sin, but that grace steps in and "overwrites" it. The passage says:

> And you were dead in the trespasses and sins in which you once walked, following the course of this world, following the prince of the power of the air, the spirit that is now at work in the sons of disobedience— among whom we all once lived in the passions of our flesh, carrying out the desires of the body and the mind, and were by nature children of wrath, like the rest of mankind. But God, being rich in mercy, because of the great love with which he loved us, even when we were dead in our trespasses, made us alive together with Christ—by grace you have been saved— and raised us up with him and seated us with him in the

heavenly places in Christ Jesus so that in the coming ages he might show the immeasurable riches of his grace in kindness toward us in Christ Jesus. For by grace you have been saved through faith. And this is not your own doing; it is the gift of God, not a result of works, so that no one may boast. For we are his workmanship, created in Christ Jesus for good works, which God prepared beforehand, that we should walk in them.

Now we put all the pieces together. What does it mean that we are "justified by God's grace"? it means that because of God's free gift, all that sin is not "counted" against us. Does that mean our natures now have no inclination toward sin and that the forces of Sin and society no longer have any sway? Unfortunately, no. It would be awesome, but it actually doesn't work like that.

With Christ in us, we have a major advantage over sin. Jesus, as you may recall, did not sin. But—and this is radical to say—he *could have*. That's the only thing that makes sense of how Jesus can be our example. Hebrews 4:15 describes Jesus this way: "For we do not have a high priest who is unable to sympathize with our weaknesses, but one who in every respect has been tempted as we are, yet without sin." The nature of Jesus in us, the Holy Spirit, gives us great power in combating the dark forces of Sin. We work with the Spirit by not conforming to the patterns of the world and by renewing our minds (Rom. 12:2).

We cannot believe nor act as if our identity is in sin, even if sin is a part of us. God has justified us. God doesn't count our sin against us. When we come to God, confessing our faults and mistakes, God sees us not as wretched but as justified. We are a new creation. The old has passed away, and the new has come (2 Cor. 5:17). As deSilva says in an-

27

other awesome work, "This description of the justified life is a description of a *transformed* life."[xii] This transformed life is marked by God's grace. Grace is a power stronger than Sin.

We *are* sinners. That's a fact. We mess up. All the time. We have all probably done some pretty bad things that we regret. We can't deny that we are constantly pulled toward evil. But, because of the blessing of God's grace, we are justified—we are counted not as sinners but as the saved! Our identity is thus no in sin, but it is in grace! We are under grace if we fellowship with God.

reflection questions

1. What are ways you see sin overstressed in the Christian culture?

2. Do you overstress your own sinful actions and thoughts?

3. What is your personal motivation for not sinning?

4. How can we make grace more a part of our identity, more than sin?

5. How does your life change when you view your identity in terms of grace and not in terms of sin?

"Try not to become a man of success but rather try to become a man of value."

Albert Einstein

chapter two

Success / Heart for God

AT the 73rd Golden Globe Awards in 2016, actor and comedian Jim Carrey gave a pointed and powerful speech, although very tongue-in-cheek. As he presented the award for best comedy or musical motion picture, he told the audience of celebrities and elites:

> I'm two-time Golden Globe winner Jim Carrey. When I go to sleep at night, I'm not just a guy going to sleep. I'm two-time Golden Globe winner Jim Carrey going to some well-needed shut eye. And when I dream, I don't dream any old dream. No sir. I dream of being three-time Golden Globe-winning actor Jim Carrey. Because then I would be enough. It would finally be true. And I can stop this terrible search. For what I know ultimately won't fulfill me.[xiii]

Jim Carrey might be joking, but he might also be on to something! Success and accomplishments have a way of very quickly becoming key aspects of our identity as we seek fulfillment. But achievement can't actually fulfill, as even the rich and successful Carrey admits.

The previous chapter confronted a distinctively Christian problem with identity. The secular world is not saying, "you are defined by sin." That's what some in the Christian world are saying. This present chapter, however, tackles a matter being said in *both* worlds—the sacred and secular.

Unfortunately, some believers have adopted the world's view on success and have imported these views into their own faith. But disastrous results follow from such a move.

success as an idol

Success is as nebulous a term as sin.

Almost always, a definition of success includes excessive stuff. Lots of money. Lots of houses. Lots of cars. Lots of influence. Lots of fans. There are many advantages to being ultra-successful, rich, and famous—whatever that looks like for you. You can take pride in your accomplishments. You have access to the fun things you want to do. People admire you for your position. You can live a comfortable life. It's all pretty grand. If a genie offers to make your wishes come true, most of us would probably use one of our wishes to ask for something along the lines of "riches, fame, or a high status." It just seems to be human nature. It only took humans eleven chapters in Genesis to build a tower together for the expressed purpose of "making a name for themselves" (11:4). What really has changed since then?

Though he wrote halfway through the 20th century, 40 years before the internet went mainstream, theologian Paul Tillich had a finger on the pulse of the Western world. He compares "success" to a kind of faith. He writes:

> It [success] is the god of many people in the highly competitive Western culture and it does what every ultimate concern must do: it demands unconditional surrender to its laws even if the price is the sacrifice of genuine human relations, personal conviction, and creative *eros*. Its threat is social and economic defeat, and its promise—indefinite as all such promises—the

fulfillment of one's being. …When fulfilled, the promise of this faith proves to be empty.[xiv]

Success, as Tillich points out, is a god. It is an idol. The addiction
to achievement in our culture is the worship of a god that is not God.
To his point, it requires sacrifice. To truly achieve something of yourself
in the modern world, chances are you are going to have to "sell your
soul." While some people can stumble into fame, others have desired it
from the start and will do almost anything to gain all those followers or
all that cash. When success becomes your sole pursuit or a primary pursuit, it becomes your identity. You live and die by some measurement of
your success. Your thoughts, actions, feelings—in other words, what
makes you unique—are filtered through the obsession.

An excellent example is a dystopian parody of the phenomenon in
the season five episode of *Community* called "App Development and
Condiments." In this episode, the community college beta tests an app
called MeowMeowBeenz. On the app, students can rate other students
one to five, five being the best. The more MeowMeowBeenz you have,
the more influential your rating of others becomes. Thus, Fives gain
notoriety, and others want to please them in order to strengthen their
own ratings. Quickly into the episode, the school has descended into a
class-based society, with the elite Fives and Fours ruling over the rest.
However, it doesn't take much for the tides to turn. Though satirical, it
is a solid commentary on the lengths people go to get popular; the
groupthink involved that strips individuality and the fickle nature of a
high position.

The story of David in Scripture is also telling. You have two wildly
different sides to David. Before he officially ascends to the throne, in 1
Samuel, David is one of the best characters in the whole Bible. David
pens memorable hymns. He fights Goliath with faith in the Lord over
faith in weapons. Time and time again, God wins battles through him.

What makes David stand above others in Scripture is his allegiance to Saul, God's anointed, *despite Saul wanting to kill him*. David has success, riches, and some power, yet he remains committed to God. However, it all changes in 2 Samuel. When David is on the throne, we see him fall from God. First, it's adultery which leads to murder. Later, he takes a census against God's wishes. Then the mighty warrior stays home instead of leading his troops. When David finally reached the pinnacle of power, even the godly, devoted, faithful David had trouble honoring God. And if you take a trip through Israel's various kings, you'll realize that a common theme is that kings are bad. It's almost expected that people in power have negative traits that don't honor God.

Yet, I realize some people have the desire for achievement but don't approach the desire with a soulless fervor. Certainly, some people want to achieve success because of a selfish need for power, though I also recognize a lot of us just want the nice comfortable life that comes with money, power, and achievement. I mean, a little comfort, a little extra spending money wouldn't be bad! Even if we aren't reaching for the top 1% of the world, many of us have desires for that comfortable life where money isn't an issue and people pay you respect. Thanks to social media, we also can peek at comfortable lifestyles very easily—or, at least, manufactures the illusion of a perfect, problem-free life. Humans don't like to have to worry about things. And if you are like me, you've rationalized the pursuit of more money because "oh, then I could give more money back."

In this day and age, hard work isn't very popular, but the desire for more stuff is popular. When you have "more," you often just have an easier, more problem-free life. This isn't just a jab at Millennials (of which I am one). Thanks to technology, many areas of our life that used to be chores 50 years ago can be done by a machine without much input. However, with more money, we can also hire more human help.

Cleaning, cooking, driving, shopping, and many daily needs can all be outsourced to someone else if you have extra cash to spend. Have you noticed that every new startup is built on the premise of having someone else do something that is a minor inconvenience in your life, like shopping or picking out your clothes or scheduling playdates?

I recognize that a lot of people who desire a little bit more in life aren't evil, purely selfish, or willing to sell their souls. But there still might be problems with the pursuit of success, even if our motivates are (mostly) pure.

Being comfortable is not bad or sinful. Living in abject poverty is not the only way to honor God (though let's be honest, a huge swath of early Christians voluntarily choose poverty because of their religious convictions). However, the achievement of a successful or comfortable lifestyle can become an idol. It can become a part of our identity in a way that distracts us from what truly matters. It's an idol in the wider culture outside the church and, in many cases, an idol in the church today. We have to constantly check ourselves to see if our casual wish for a comfortable life ends up taking over a part of our identity reserved for God.

A great example of the good guy with success as a crunch occurs in the Gospels of Matthew, Mark, and Luke. Here we find a character often called the Rich Young Ruler. The narrative demonstrates that wealth and achievements can become major crutches for us in our lives, even if we are generally good people. It points out the difficulties in trying to follow Jesus *and* success. You can find this conversation in Mark 10:17-22.

> And as he was setting out on his journey, a man ran up
> and knelt before him and asked him, "Good Teacher,
> what must I do to inherit eternal life?" And Jesus said
> to him, "Why do you call me good? No one is good ex-

cept God alone. You know the commandments: 'Do not murder, Do not commit adultery, Do not steal, Do not bear false witness, Do not defraud, Honor your father and mother.'" And he said to him, "Teacher, all these I have kept from my youth." And Jesus, looking at him, loved him, and said to him, "You lack one thing: go, sell all that you have and give to the poor, and you will have treasure in heaven; and come, follow me." Disheartened by the saying, he went away sorrowful, for he had great possessions.

You can imagine that the rich young ruler was expecting affirmation. After the exchange, the rich dude is disheartened. He went in feeling confident because he hasn't murdered anyone, hasn't committed adultery, and he honors his father and mother like no one else! This character is fascinating because he represents so many Christians I know. A lot of believers go to church, don't really do major bad stuff, have given money to at least one charity, and they think they got it. I've been in that spot loads of time. On paper, the rich young ruler is practically perfect. But Jesus isn't asking us to be perfect on paper. He's demanding more.

Let's finish with what Jesus says in response to this. In a classic Jesus-move, Jesus turns this into a teaching moment. Mark 10:23-27 continues:

And Jesus looked around and said to his disciples, "How difficult it will be for those who have wealth to enter the kingdom of God!" And the disciples were amazed at his words. But Jesus said to them again, "Children, how difficult it is to enter the kingdom of God! It is easier for a camel to go through the eye of a needle than for a rich person to enter the kingdom of God." And they were exceedingly astonished, and said to him, "Then who can be saved?" Jesus looked at them and said, "With man it is impossible, but not with God. For all things are possible with God."

Jesus affirms that those with a lot of possession have a hard time getting into the Kingdom. He says a camel going through the eye of the needle will have an easier time. Whether this refers to the "eye" of a sewing needle or it is a nickname for a short gate in Jerusalem, the point is that the rich, the ones with the most to lose, have a difficult road ahead of them. One clue about Jesus' analogy is in the crowd's reaction. They wonder how ANYONE can be saved if even a good rich guy with all the comforts of life is going to have a challenge. Rich, poor, whatever—getting into the Kingdom is not a walk in the park.

Of course, if you are wealthy, that doesn't mean you CAN'T ever get into the Kingdom of God. As Jesus says: with God, all things are possible! But this does reveal that wealth gets our priorities out of whack. This ruler followed all the commandments, but he lacked a few really important aspects of righteousness like giving, selflessness, helping others. It seemed like he had in his faith for HIMSELF and not God. He put his identity in achievements—both his wealth and his ability to follow the commandments.

false idol

It is appropriate to look at what the Bible says about wealth, success, and comfort when it comes to our identities. Scripture has a wide variety of views on the subject.

On the one hand, you see the Proverbs view on wealth, where righteousness pays off with a monetary blessing. We read that Solomon also got riches, power, and success thrown in because he demonstrated wisdom in requesting wisdom as his one request from God. Then there is the Job version, where even though the lesson is that your success is not tied to your righteousness, the ending still includes Job being rewarded for his faithfulness by getting back double of everything he had previously owned.

But against these stories and texts is a much deeper thread that runs in the Old and New Testaments that challenges our notions of success. Though some parts of Scripture make it seem like righteousness births success or that it's not really bad to be comfortable, plenty of other parts critique these notions. Let's look at a few of those critiques.

A major problem with wealth is that it is ultimately unreliable. The unnamed Preacher in Ecclesiastes has several opinions on what is truly valuable. In Ecclesiastes 5:10-15, the wizened educator says:

> He who loves money will not be satisfied with money, nor he who loves wealth with his income; this also is vanity. When goods increase, they increase who eat them, and what advantage has their owner but to see them with his eyes? Sweet is the sleep of a laborer, whether he eats little or much, but the full stomach of the rich will not let him sleep.
>
> There is a grievous evil that I have seen under the sun: riches were kept by their owner to his hurt, and those riches were lost in a bad venture. And he is father of a son, but he has nothing in his hand. As he came from his mother's womb he shall go again, naked as he came, and shall take nothing for his toil that he may carry away in his hand.

Having lots of money is usually thought of as the ultimate safety net. There's an anecdote that Bill Gates would waste his time picking up a $100 bill he dropped since he makes ways more than $100 in the few seconds leaning down to pick it up. While Gates might be fine, the reality is that money isn't always a sure safety net. Your money or possessions can be taken away. Unexpected medical bills, crashes in the stock market, or poor investments in your cousin's new business venture can all suck us dry. If you've invested your identity in how much stuff you have or in your comfortable lifestyle, what will you do if all that is suddenly stripped away?

Yet the Preacher reminds that even if you keep your possessions all your life, in the end, your achievements and stuff don't even matter. You can't take it with you! A camp skit from the 5th and 6th-grade Christian summer camp I attended took this idea and played it out comedically. An actor would be climbing up the stairs carrying imaginary things. Other actors would ask: "What's that?" The other would reply that they were storing items in the attic so they could grab them when they died and were floating up to Heaven. They stored roller-skates for the pearly streets, or skis for the snow-topped Mount Zion, and a kayak for the crystal seas. At the end of the skit, the person falls off the ladder. The others immediately run up the ladder to see if the stuff is gone. It's still there, they say. One of them wonders if instead of going up…he went down. It's all a funny joke, but the lesson that "you can't take it with you" is nonetheless true.

breaking the idol of success

Jesus does preach about storing up treasures in Heaven, but it's not about skis or roller-stakes. Preaching in Matthew 6:19-21, Jesus teaches: "Do not lay up for yourselves treasures on earth, where moth and rust destroy and where thieves break in and steal, but lay up for yourselves treasures in heaven, where neither moth nor rust destroys and where thieves do not break in and steal. For where your treasure is, there your heart will be also." We are supposed to store our "treasures"—focus our efforts—not on accumulating "stuff" here on earth but accumulating metaphorical "stuff" in Heaven.

Jesus is trying to get us to change our hearts. The stuff you collect on earth, the achievements you add to your LinkedIn, the success you have that brings the crowds swarming to you—none of that matters in light of Heaven. Now, unlike the way many philosophers of Jesus' day thought, the things of this earth are not *bad* or *evil*. Earth isn't evil or something to not care about all. Yet, we do well to remember that anything the world provides has no comparison to the Kingdom of God. Jesus is suggesting we need a new approach, a new attitude.

Now, as I've alluded to earlier, I think one of the reasons we are tempted to focus on gathering material on earth is comfort, safety, and security (as opposed to pure greed). And a concern for those things at all times often leads to worry. Jesus' major speech on worrying in Matthew 6 is often detached from its context: however, he is still talking about money here. It's not too long after the previous discussion about the proper location to store your treasures. Jesus starts the conversation by saying, "No one can serve two masters, for either he will hate the one and love the other, or he will be devoted to the one and despise the other. You cannot serve God and money" (Matt. 6:24). Then Bible translations usually cut it off and title the next section "Do Not Be Anxious" or something similar. But in this case, it seems Jesus is building off his point about who/what masters you when he talks about worrying—notice that "therefore" at the beginning. Jesus continues in Matthew 6:25-34 on this subject:

> Therefore I tell you, do not be anxious about your life,
> what you will eat or what you will drink, nor about your
> body, what you will put on. Is not life more than food,
> and the body more than clothing? Look at the birds of

the air: they neither sow nor reap nor gather into barns, and yet your heavenly Father feeds them. Are you not of more value than they? And which of you by being anxious can add a single hour to his span of life? And why are you anxious about clothing? Consider the lilies of the field, how they grow: they neither toil nor spin, yet I tell you, even Solomon in all his, glory was not arrayed like one of these. But if God so clothes the grass of the field, which today is alive and tomorrow is thrown into the oven, will he not much more clothe you, O you of little faith? Therefore do not be anxious, saying, 'What shall we eat?' or 'What shall we drink?' or 'What shall we wear?' For the Gentiles seek after all these things, and your heavenly Father knows that you need them all. But seek first the kingdom of God and his righteousness, and all these things will be added to you. Therefore do not be anxious about tomorrow, for tomorrow will be anxious for itself. Sufficient for the day is its own trouble.

Jesus offers a formula simple in theory but incredibly difficult in practice: "seek first the kingdom of God and his righteousness, and all these things will be added to you."

Earlier in this same chapter, Jesus had discussed how to pray and had suggested the line "Give us this day our daily bread" (6:11). Theologian Stanley Hauerwas notes how this prayer changes us. He writes,

Without the community that Jesus has called into existence, we are tempted to hoard, to store up resources, in a vain effort to ensure safety and security. Of course our effort to live without risk not only results in injus-

tice, but it also makes our own lives anxious, fearing
that we never have enough.[xv]

Hauerwas refers to this temptation for more as wanting "the bread
of the devil." Jesus, conversely, compels us to ask for no more than our
daily bread.

So don't worry about your comfort or safety. Instead, focus on
honoring God. God gives us enough. The idea of "seeking first the
kingdom of God" means to prioritize your Creator above everything
else, above material and social success that seems to offer meaning to
our lives. Fame and fortune must not be your primary aim in life—it
probably shouldn't even be in your Top Ten life goals. Instead of putting your identity in success, put your identity in having a heart for God.

Discussing instructions for the rich, 1 Timothy 6:17-19 nicely
summarizes everything discussed so far. Paul offers good advice to everyone, especially those already with worldly success.

> As for the rich in this present age, charge them not to
> be haughty, nor to set their hopes on the uncertainty of
> riches, but on God, who richly provides us with eve-
> rything to enjoy. They are to do good, to be rich in
> good works, to be generous and ready to share,
> thus storing up treasure for themselves as a good
> foundation for the future, so that they may take hold
> of that which is truly life.

When our lives are built around heavenly treasures, we gain a
whole new perspective. We must keep our "eyes on the prize," so to
speak, and not let distractions of life, distractions that claim to give life
yet keep us from the real goal. What we do on earth is important, of
course, but what is most important is not what we build with our hands
but what we build with our hearts. We must strive to honor God and

not honor ourselves. Our identities are found in what our heart most longs for, and as Christian, that is supposed to be God.

You are not your stuff. You are not your achievements. You are not the numbers in your bank account. In truth, in God's eyes, you are not defined by any worldly success. Instead, our identity should be rooted in having a heart for God. What should shape your life is a commitment to seeking after God, to storing treasures up in Heaven, not on earth. We strive after Jesus and not comfort. That is who we are called to be as followers of God. We have a different system of priorities compared to the world. We have a unique aim and direction. We have a new heart.

reflection questions

1. What are ways you see success overstressed in culture, both in the church and outside of it?
2. Do you have a problem with overvaluing success?
3. What does it look like to "store treasures in Heaven?"
4. What does it look like to "seek first the Kingdom of God?"
5. How does your life change when you view your identity in terms of your heart for God and not in terms of success?

"Life can only be understood
backwards; but it must be lived
forwards."

Søren Kierkegaard

chapter three

Past / Future Promise

WHY does it seem like every contemporary novel is about a guy or girl "haunted by their past?" It's a trope to add a sense of mystery to the story, but perhaps it reveals something else about human nature. A lot of people relate to having a problem with the past. The average person doesn't human their life's story on random strangers. It takes time to reveal your past to someone— whether that past is that you were a secret agent or if your past is filled with familial trauma.

People have regrets about choices they made or things they've said even years and years after. I don't think it's just me, but I can exactly remember things I've seen, said, and done from my early years, even when I've forgotten most of what I learned about math in high school. The past affects us today—we can't escape that. Maybe your past has stripped away earthly advantages for you in life. Maybe your past keeps haunting you, reminding you of what you've done or what's been done to you. Many people carry with them into the future a wide assortment of trauma from the past.

Our relationship with our pasts can often be very dicey. Some simply move on while others can't help but hold on. Dangerously, our past can too often inappropriately define our present identity. But as Christians, our identity is not rooted in our personal past but in the future promise.

haunted by the past

It's undeniable that one of the first ways we self-identity is to construct an identity based on our "past." Our parents or guardians shape our personality. We learn things as a kid and keep them with us. Have you ever had an experience where you go to someone else's house and were "amazed" that they did something different? We tend to think some of the behaviors present in our upbringing are normal and just like everyone else. It's not until you spent the night at someone else's house, or have a roommate in college, or get married, that you figure out what's "normal" to you isn't normal to everyone else, even in the little things. I push my toothpaste out near its neck; my wife pushes toothpaste out from the bottom of the tube. We each think the other is doing it weird.

Biographies are very obvious ways where an author explains how a person "came to be." Autobiographies, even more so, tap into a person's history and psyche to try to explain a person later in life. This kind of project is a helpful project. We cannot deny the effect that our place of childhood, the character of our parents, the worldview of our schools, and more have on us. Starting a biography right at the moment where a famous person succeeded in being notable would be really strange and perhaps meaningless. Though it is not often at the forefront of our minds, we know that great achievements and notoriety don't just come out of thin air—various forces, both external and internal, shape us.

The past creates us, but it doesn't have to define us. My personality is shaped by the family I was raised in, but I can make a conscious effort to be a different person than my family. I control my identity. This isn't being "rebellious," but growing in my own personality and in growing toward God. Even if your upbringing was great and you have many happy experiences, it shouldn't necessarily define you. God calls us beyond identification in our past. Like we discussed with sin and grace, God is concerned mostly with who we are now, not where we've come from.

However your past impacts your life now, the past clearly matters. But I want to propose a Biblical response for our relationship with our personal histories. I want to suggest that our identities should not be formed around what we've done or what's been done to us but should be formed around our *future* promise from God. The story of Scripture calls us in this direction.

Yet what happens when we despise those forces of the past? What happens when moments from our history are seared onto our brain? What about when we try to move on from a past identity, but those convictions of the past still haunt us? Where do we go from here? What do we do when the past lingers and haunts us?

There are complicated questions. This chapter is no substitute for therapy or good, hard discussions with loved ones. You will have to decide what practices and habits best help you overcome life's turmoil while recognizing the course that has made you who you *you*. However, Scripture offers us the motivation to make these important moves from the past to the future.

the prostitute, pained, and the persecutor

Three characters in the Bible who put off their past identities and looked forward into the future will be our guides as we pave a way to understanding a Biblical response. Each of these people represents a different relationship with the past, so if you don't see yourself in one, you may see yourself in another. But even if none of them speak to your situation, surely the real lesson is that God accepts broken people and invites them to participate in a better future.

There are a lot of different places to start on this quest. I want to begin with a woman in the Bible who doesn't get nearly enough credit for her part in the history of God's people. Let's spotlight Rahab. We learn from Joshua 2 that Rahab is a prostitute, yet she hides the Israelite spies and lies to her own people to protect them. Once the men of Jericho go on a wild goose chase, she speaks to the spies. She says she knows the Lord has given the whole land to Israel. She has heard the stories of God's might and power. She admits her own people are scared of them. So she asks that because of her kindness to the spies, that your family and all who belong to them will be saved (Josh. 2:12-13). They agree.

The text lacks a detailed back story for Rahab. And as is typical with the Bible, we barely get a peek into her inner psychological workings. But we know she's smart enough (or scared enough) to recognize the power of the Lord. She sides with the random former slaves that have waltzed into her ancestral land over and against the city of her people. A bold lady! We also can guess she cares about her family. She isn't just striking a deal for her own safety. Her family is important to her as well.

Yet, she's also a prostitute. Many translations use the harsher word "harlot." Rahab is a sex worker, a job with a complicated reputation. Biblical scholar Phyllis Bird explains, "Her social status is that of an outcast, though not an outlaw, a tolerated, but dishonored member of society."[xvi] She clearly did well enough to own her own home (it's possible she also runs an inn) and have some agency in society. Yet she lives against the wall of the town, on the outskirts, where the outcasts lived. Yes, she is practically the literal definition of an outcast. Extrabiblical Jewish tradition says that Rahab had been a prostitute for 40 years—since she was 10—and at 50 became a believer in Yahweh.[xvii]

Obviously, prostitution is not an allowable profession according to Hebrew law. Prostitutes were shamed, ostracized, and sometimes even killed. Even if you ignored the religious side of things—prostitution was sometimes thought to threaten the political system because it could break apart families, which were the fundamentally most important part of ancient societies. Here in the story, though, we have no mention of her occupation being a good or bad thing. It just *is*. Yet with the backdrop of the rest of Scripture, an ancient reader would certainly be shocked to find this harlot helping the Hebrews. This prostitute acknowledges God—and jaws would drop. Many early Jewish commentators heralded Rahab as the great example of a Gentile coming into the fold of Judaism, rejecting her sinful life and embracing God.

Though little is known of her life, her occupation and reputation surely defined her for years. But her lasting legacy is not in her past but in her choice to not let social stigmas dictate her life. In *The Encyclopedia of Jewish Women*, Tikva Frymer-Kensky points out just how important this prostitute is to Israel's story: "Rahab is thus the oracle of Israel's occupation of the land. ... Rahab, who begins as triply marginalized—Canaanite, woman, and prostitute—moves to the center as bearer of a divine message and herald of Israel in its new land."[xviii] Hebrews 11:31 remembers her by saying, "By faith Rahab, the prostitute, did not perish with those who were disobedient, because she had given a friendly welcome to the spies." It's interesting she is still recalled as a prostitute, but I suspect the mention of her scandalous occupation is there to highlight how, through faith, we too can fight back from the stereotypes of our former life. We can overcome the past and make for ourselves a better future.

We have no real clue about Rahab's life before the spies, but it probably wasn't living anything like what God wanted. However, later in life, she became convicted by the power of God. She changed. She could have been too ashamed to help the Israelites, but she wasn't. She didn't let her past keep her from creating a better future for herself. Not only did she and her family survive, but her faith continues to be an example to people even today. She's in the genealogy of Jesus, and Jewish tradition also puts her as the ancestor of several notable prophets and a group of priests. Rahab knows what it's like to cast off, placing her identity in her past and being redefined by God.

Our next character study is David. He, of course, gets a lot of attention at church because he's pretty cool, and he monopolizes a good chunk of 1 and 2 Samuel. Obviously, the whole David and Goliath deal is an early triumph for him—it's a favorite story to tell. But even with that success and the other battles he won, David quickly found himself in trouble. Thanks to his popularity, the current King, Saul, really found him threatening. Saul straight-up wanted David dead. Thus, David had to go on the run, separated from his best friend Jonathan while his friend's dad tried to kill him. What a life.

As the dramatic David is prone to do, he wrote several psalms during this experience to encapsulate with words the emotions he felt. Psalm 142, just seven verses, is said to have been written by David while he hid in a cave turning this troublesome time. He writes:

> With my voice I cry out to the Lord;
>> with my voice I plead for mercy to the Lord.
> I pour out my complaint before him;
>> I tell my trouble before him.
> When my spirit faints within me,
>> you know my way!
> In the path where I walk
>> they have hidden a trap for me.
> Look to the right and see:
>> there is none who takes notice of me;

no refuge remains to me;

    no one cares for my soul.

I cry to you, O Lord;

    I say, "You are my refuge,

    my portion in the land of the living."

Attend to my cry,

    for I am brought very low!

Deliver me from my persecutors,

    for they are too strong for me!

Bring me out of prison,

    that I may give thanks to your name!

The righteous will surround me,

    for you will deal bountifully with me.

David is feeling lost, conflict, possibly even depressed. He is struggling with God at this time because he is being hunted for literally nothing. Saul wants to kill him simply because *David is so good at his job*. Now David wrestles with what to do with a seemingly distant God and a difficult path ahead of him.

Certainly, David did have many advantages in his life, but he also had many hardships. Even after his life on the run, his best friend was killed, his father-in-law was killed (he was sad at Saul's death despite Saul not liking him), and he eventually lost a baby. David's life was filled with death and difficulty. Certainly, as king, he had some significant flaws, but overall he created a lasting legacy as a man after God's Own Heart. But instead of pressing on to successes, he could have lived in the feeling of Psalm 142. In his time prior to King, he didn't deserve a lot of that trouble—yet the world, at least parts of it, were literally out to get him!

The mighty warrior persevered despite these early challenges. He didn't give up on God nor on his mission in life. He continued to (mostly) make God-honoring choices. Later in life, after being rescued from

51

Saul's clutches, David writes Psalm 18. I encourage you to read the whole chapter, but here are the first three lines:

> I love you, O Lord, my strength.
>
>   The Lord is my rock and my fortress and my deliverer,
> my God, my rock, in whom I take refuge,
>
>   my shield, and the horn of my salvation, my stronghold.
> I call upon the Lord, who is worthy to be praised,
>
>   and I am saved from my enemies.

Even when life threw a lot of bad at him for no good reason, David was later able to see that God protected him. At the moment, while hiding out in a cave, fearing that one of the most powerful people in the land would kill him, he had trouble wrestling with his situation. Yet, with a bit of perspective, he could see the truth: God was with him. He didn't need to be a man trapped in a troubled path; he could move on and praise God.

Our last character had an incredible life change—a totally 180-degree turn. Second, only to Jesus in the New Testament, Paul is a major force in early Christianity. But he wasn't always that champion of the way of Jesus. In fact, he used to be against everything that followers of Jesus stood for—to the point of killing these women and men. Acts record the account of his version many times. On one occasion, he reflects on his past as a ruler in Acts 26:9-11. Paul recalls:

> I myself was convinced that I ought to do many things
> in opposing the name of Jesus of Nazareth. And I did
> so in Jerusalem. I not only locked up many of the saints
> in prison after receiving authority from the chief
> priests, but when they were put to death, I cast my
> vote against them. And I punished them often in all
> the synagogues and tried to make them blaspheme,

and in raging fury against them I persecuted them
even to foreign cities.

When Jesus miraculously appeared to him, as recorded in Acts 9, Paul is forced to confront his actions. He obeys the call of Jesus and turns over a whole new leaf. Instead of bringing letters to persecute the Christians, he brings to his own people, the Jewish people who refused to follow Jesus, the news that Christ suffered for our sins and demands repentance.

Of course, radical change is often met with skepticism. When Paul converted, those from his former life and those who identified along with him would have been skeptical. The text tells us as much. In Acts 9:20-22.

For some days, he was with the disciples at Damascus. And immediately, he proclaimed Jesus in the synagogues, saying, "He is the Son of God." And all who heard him were amazed and said, "Is not this the man who made havoc in Jerusalem of those who called upon this name? And has he not come here for this purpose, to bring them bound before the chief priests?" But Saul increased all the more in strength and confounded the Jews who lived in Damascus by proving that Jesus was the Christ.

Some of his Jewish brethren even reach the point of planning to kill him! Luckily, Paul's disciples get word of the plan, and they sneak him out of Damascus. When Paul arrives in Jerusalem, however, his new believing buddies had a hard time accepting him. "And when he had come to Jerusalem, he attempted to join the disciples. And they were all afraid of him, for they did not believe that he was a disciple" (Acts 9:26). Imagine being Paul, having to live with the fact that you put to death people for holding a belief that you know hold, yet he is rejected on all sides.

Paul had an interesting past. To his fellow Jewish Pharisees, he might have been a hero for his persecution of Christian heretics. It's easy to see he really misunderstood what the new Jesus movement was all about, and he definitely misunderstood what his Jewish faith demanded of him. But once he got his life and thinking in order, he put that same zeal into a more productive avenue: spreading the Gospel! A way better thing to do. Paul's past could have haunted him. It would be easy to see him suggesting that his past invalidated him from being a part of the Christian faith in the future. Lucky for us, Paul did not place his identity in the things he did in the past. He let God bestow upon him a new identity as a messenger of God.

being future-focused

The three characters were supposed to illustrate what I see as three kinds of "pasts" we can have that might affect us today. Rahab had a past where she did bad things, but she didn't let that stop her from doing good. David had a past where bad things were done to him, but he didn't let that stop him from success. Paul had a past where he strongly believed in ideals that made him do bad things, but when he changed his mind, he didn't let that hold him back from his new mission.

Our stories can likely be found in one of these places. Maybe you lived a wild and sinful life and now have trouble starting a good path forward. Perhaps you have been a victim—through no fault of your own—to hardship, abuse, rape, bullying, death, and the cruelty of life. Where do you go from here when life has taken, taken, taken, and hardly gives? For others, you might sympathize with Paul, who thought his beliefs were solid and his actions legitimate, yet then he has to face the fact that for so many years, he was wrong. Each of these characters, however, did not let the past define their future.

There is something all three have in common: they look forward to the future, specifically the future promises that God delivered. Rahab had faith in an invisible God that she and her family would be protected in the future battle. David had the promise of kingship to look forward to. Paul was given a very specific mission: that he would be a light to the Gentiles. To deal with their pasts, they grounded themselves in the future beyond the horizons, which they could do because of unshakable faith in God's provision.

Paul describes this process very well in Philippians 3. After going through an impressive resume (which includes that he was "a persecutor of the church"), he declares in verse 8, "Indeed, I count everything as loss because of the surpassing worth of knowing Christ Jesus my Lord. For his sake, I have suffered the loss of all things and count them as rubbish, in order that I may gain Christ." He throws away his resume to gain Christ. Then he lays out a plan for every Christian to follow:

> Not that I have already obtained this or am already perfect, but I press on to make it my own, because Christ Jesus has made me his own. Brothers [and sisters], I do not consider that I have made it my own. But one thing I do: forgetting what lies behind and straining forward to what lies ahead, I press on toward the goal for the prize of the upward call of God in Christ Jesus. Let those of us who are mature think this way, and if in anything you think otherwise, God will reveal that also to you. Only let us hold true to what we have attained (Phil. 3:12-16).

Cast off what lies behind and look forward to the prize. There is light at the end of the tunnel. Our prize is communion with God in Christ Jesus. Day after day, we struggle, like the Apostle Paul, to attain this prize. It is not easy to place our identity in a future we can't clearly see, founded upon faith, promised by a God that doesn't always clue us into the grand plan. But we press on toward Jesus because Christ Jesus has made us his own. When Christ defines us, he defines us not in terms of our past but in our future promise.

Our pasts undeniably play a role in our lives. But in our lives, a larger role should go to our future promise. We are not ultimately defined by who we were but by who we will become. Let us together press on to the future goal, putting away how we used to act, what was done to us, and how we used to think. Let us strive toward the Promised Land, a land we won't reach until our days on earth are done.

reflection questions

1. What are examples of people in pop culture or in your own lives who are defined by things they have done in their past?

2. What experiences in your past have made it difficult to live a life honoring God?

3. What experiences in your past have made you a *better* person?

4. Do you more identify with Rahab with her sinful past, David who was mistreated by others, or Paul who build a life on a false idea?

5. How does your life change when you view your identity in terms of the future promise and not in terms of your own past?

"Love is that condition in which
the happiness of another person
is essential to your own."
Robert Heinlein

chapter four

Happiness / Helping Others

WHAT is something that makes you happy?

I have to admit, there is something about my cat that sparks joy like none others. While I don't feel this about all cats, there is something about *my* cat that is special. It's not what he does or even how he looks. It's just that my cat, Simon, naturally seems to radiate cuteness. Whether he's laying there, or playing with string, or snuggling, it just makes me happy. Even when he misbehaves, man, it's hard to stay mad at him. All other forms of entertainment seem to let me down, but even when my cat isn't doing something, it puts a smile on my face.

Pets, songs, movies, hobbies, art, intellectual stimulation—there are a variety of things that might make you happy in this day and age. One person's happiness may not be the same for another, but all of us tend to have *something* that brightens our day and gives us a burst of energy. Even the most miserable people can find some spark of happiness to give a little dopamine rush. There certainly is no shortage of entertainment in the Western world! At practically any moment, we can entertain ourselves.

the pursuit of happiness

Being happy is a really great thing. Generally speaking, we want to be happy. Typically, no one is asking for more pain, more frustration, more insecurity, and more danger in their lives. In America, our Constitution even takes it for granted that "the pursuit of happiness" is an "unaliena-ble right." Our world today seems to mostly be set-up to increase our personal well-being—there are tools, toys, and services that have no other use than to make us happier. The self-help industry is booming, with new books, videos, podcasts, and blogs being released all the time to help us live life with a smile on our faces. Life hacks travel the Inter-net at light speed, saving us precious seconds on mundane daily tasks. Today, happiness is a valuable commodity that we use to trade with, whether we know it or not.

Right now, the world is the most prosperous, healthiest, and vio-lence-free that it has ever been in history—but even in several of the "developed" countries, happiness is on the decline, and mental health problems are on the rise. For being a happiness-obsessed society—we just aren't all that happy. There are a lot of theories out there; there are a lot of things to blame. Yet, we simply don't know the answer to this conundrum. What is obvious, nevertheless, is that something is wrong. Somehow, with all the perks of modern life, we've failed to achieve hap-piness and fullness of life. Even still, so many are obsessed with self-fulfillment. Far too many people have built their identity on always be-ing happy and satisfied with their life.

If you pressed me to name the problem, I might venture to say that it's actually our individualistic selfishness that is truly hurting us. If you pressed me to name the solution, I have to ultimately point to the Chris-tian faith, which is the best (though not only) answer to the issue. Be-coming a Christian doesn't "poof" away from the problems, but it does provide a set of solutions to navigate the issues.

It is only logical to turn to the unnamed author and narrator of Ec-clesiastes. This "Preacher" goes on an epic journey to find the meaning of life. But quickly, the experiment provided troubling results. In Eccle-siastes 2:10-11, the speaker summarizes his experiment and says:

And whatever my eyes desired I did not keep from them. I kept my heart from no pleasure, for my heart found pleasure in all my toil, and this was my reward for all my toil. Then I considered all that my hands had done and the toil I had expended in doing it, and behold, all was vanity and a striving after wind, and there was nothing to be gained under the sun.

At the conclusion of this great period of pleasure—where he denied himself nothing he desired—the Preacher concludes that seeking pleasure and comfort is ultimately meaningless. It never really fills the void. While later in the book, the Preacher cosigns to eating and drinking and being merry because everything is meaningless, the Preacher never becomes a libertine, a one who just does whatever makes her happy with no regard to anything else. At the end of the day, the Preacher proclaims in the last chapter of the book, following God is what matters (Ecc. 12:13-14). There you go. The answer. Easy, right?

You may have heard this phrase used: "God wants me to be happy." This is a curious statement for a variety of reasons, not the least because it is often employed as an excuse to sin. It is safe to say that God gave us desires. We are designed to want pleasure and joy, and fulfillment. It is a part of our humanity and maybe even a part of "the image of God" that is in us—after all, God created us for God's own pleasure. However, according to the Christian faith, happiness is not the end goal of life. We are not the center of the universe. There is no promise for a problem-free life (Jesus actually promises the opposite in John 16:33). An identity built on *our* own happiness is not a firm foundation that Jesus would give a thumbs up. Against the grain of this movement in our current culture, we are called to reach out to others beyond us.

Christians do not ignore happiness, but we do reframe what it means. Pleasure and happiness, as the Preacher noted, do not properly fill us up. Only God can do this; more specifically, a pursuit of godly living can fill us. As Jesus teaches in his famous collection of Beatitudes (Matt. 5:3-12), there is a blessing for God-honoring behavior.

> Blessed are the poor in spirit, for theirs is the kingdom of heaven.
>
> Blessed are those who mourn, for they shall be comforted.
>
> Blessed are the meek, for they shall inherit the earth.
>
> Blessed are those who hunger and thirst for righteousness, for they shall be satisfied.
>
> Blessed are the merciful, for they shall receive mercy.
>
> Blessed are the pure in heart, for they shall see God.
>
> Blessed are the peacemakers, for they shall be called sons of God.
>
> Blessed are those who are persecuted for righteousness' sake, for theirs is the kingdom of heaven.
>
> Blessed are you when others revile you and persecute you and utter all kinds of evil against you falsely on my account. Rejoice and be glad, for your reward is great in heaven, for so they persecuted the prophets who were before you.

We tend to get caught in the reward that comes with the attitude, but the real reward of Christian living is in the act itself—we find our blessing in living out God's true design for us. Pleasure and happiness *are* welcome in our lives. Jesus had lots of dinner parties, let's not forget! That's just not the end of the story for the people of God.

the turn toward others

One command that summarizes so much of the Old Testament and New Testament is the command to "love your neighbor as yourself."

It's not something that Jesus invented, despite what we are sometimes lead to believe. This phrase is codified in Jewish law. Leviticus 19:18 tells Israel, "you shall love your neighbor as yourself." This concept forms the basis for so much of how Israel was to structure their society and live a daily life. In the New Testament, Jesus continues this theme. Jesus' life and ministry intensify this command and make it the norm for Christian living.

While the phrase is simple, doing it is hard. In Luke 10:25-37, Jesus tells a familiar but powerful story to explain what this means in our lives. Most with some experience in faith communities know the story. Jesus describes a man beaten and thrown to the side of the road. Two religious leaders pass by until, finally, a Samaritan man helps the guy out. Samaritans and Jews were not on the best terms, but we see the Samaritan looking past all of that to reach out to someone else in need. The Samaritan even spends his own money to get the person help and shelter. We call this parable the "Good Samaritan," perhaps because, in this time period, Samaritans were not always thought to be good.

The Samaritan's goodness shines thought in his stellar actions, in the fact that he looked beyond his own interests to someone else—someone different than him, someone who would be a hassle to help. He stepped out of his comfort zone because of a higher standard than self-preservation. Jesus tells the story to explain "who" a neighbor is. The story reveals that your neighbor is *anyone* who requires your assistance. That cuts across boundary lines like race or economics or religion. Everyone is your neighbor. As Jesus says in Matthew 5:44, "Love your enemies and pray for those who persecute you." The story of the Samaritan shows, however, that love is not just "well-wishes" but leads to action in improving someone's life. Love costs something. It cost the Samaritan time, money, and safety—three favorite commodities in our contemporary culture!

Granted, it is no simple task to manufacture love for our neighbor. Developing selflessness is literally goes against every ounce of self-preservation inside of us. One issue that I see people have with developing the practice of selflessness is that they think it starts in the mind and heart. You have to *feel* compelled to help others or be *aware* that other people are in need. Then they get nowhere in the pursuit of virtuous living because manufacturing feelings and thoughts is an incredibly difficult task. So, what is the solution?

In C.S. Lewis' *Mere Christianity*, he gives a fine description of what it means to love and how to develop this practice. In his chapter on the Christian virtue of charity, he says: "Charity means 'Love, in the Christian sense.' But love, in the Christian sense, does not mean an emotion. It is a state not of the feelings but of the will; that state of the will which we have naturally about ourselves, and must learn to have about other people."[xix] Because of this definition, he goes on to encourage: "Do not waste time bothering whether you 'love' your neighbour; act as if you did. As soon as we do this we find one of the great secrets. When you are behaving as if you loved someone, you will presently come to love him. If you injure someone you dislike, you will find yourself disliking him more. If you do him a good turn, you will find yourself disking him less."[xx] For Lewis, the action is more important than the "feeling" behind it. Yet, the repeated action that goes against your natural desires starts to form a new spirit within you. As my high school drama teacher would say, "Fake it, 'till you make it."

Throwing off the old and putting on the new is no easy task, especially when the "new" is "created after the likeness of God in true righteousness and holiness" (see Eph. 4:22-24). That is a serious transformation! To master Christian love, we have to remember the source: God. In the *Imitation of Christ*, medieval theologian Thomas á Kempis describes a person with "perfect" charity, casting a vision of ideal Christian behavior:

he who has true and perfect charity seeks self in nothing, but searches all things for the glory of God. Moreover, he envies no man, because he desires no personal pleasure nor does he wish to rejoice in himself; rather he desires the greater glory of God above all things. He ascribes to man nothing that is good but attributes it wholly to God from Whom all things proceed as from a fountain, and in Whom all the blessed shall rest as their last end and fruition. If man had but a spark of true charity he would surely sense that all the things of earth are full of vanity![xxi]

Perfect charity is not easily attainable, but it is a goal we should try to attain. We will lack perfection in this act while in the current life, but one day we can attain true charity. In the process of mastering charity, it requires us to look beyond our own situation and to the greater goals of God. In the words of John the Baptist, Christ "must increase, but I must decrease" (John 3:30).

love as an identity

Most of us know that helping others is something we are supposed to do. Helping and loving others certainly gets a lot of sermon time. But I have never heard anyone suggest that helping others is a part of our IDENTITY. Yet, so much of living out our faith involves helping others. As has been noted, loving your neighbor is a central command, and it necessitates loving others over and against the things that make you happy and comfortable. Helping others is integral to what it means to be Christ-like and to have a Christian witness in the world.

We find ample proof of this in Philippians 2. In this passage, Paul includes what is sometimes called a "Christ hymn." Some scholars think the poetic saying (in v. 5-11) might be one of the oldest parts of the New Testament—a "creed" that they taught and sang—and Paul choose to include it here to develop his ideas about being Christ-like. But before the creedal statement about Jesus, Paul urges the Philippians to shape up their minds and behaviors. Philippians 2:1-5a reads:

> So if there is any encouragement in Christ, any comfort from love, any participation in the Spirit, any affection and sympathy, complete my joy by being of the same mind, having the same love, being in full accord and of one mind. Do nothing from selfish ambition or conceit, but in humility count others more significant than yourselves. Let each of you look not only to his own interests, but also to the interests of others. Have this mind among yourselves, which is yours in Christ Jesus...

The call to unity is rooted in counting other people as more significant than ourselves. It is all pretty straightforward. The "mind" of Christ is one geared toward others and not toward the pursuit of our own individual happiness.

Paul continues by describing Jesus in Philippians 2:6-11. He says that Christ "though he was in the form of God, did not count equality with God a thing to be grasped, but emptied himself, by taking the form of a servant" (Phil. 2:6-7). There is a lot of language that deserves some unpacking, but for now, I want to highlight the movement of the passage. Jesus came from a place of power and prestige to the lowly state of a servant, which came with a hefty dose of suffering. But that humility turned into exultation. Jesus gives up all, even "equality with God" (having all the powers and privileges and pain-free existence of God).

We always want to self-medicate our pain—be that with money, food, alcohol, porn, social media, or whatever. But the only medicine

66

that will give us true joy among the bad stuff of life is Jesus. Yet simply "feeling loved" by Jesus is not enough, nor is it what we are called to do. True fulfillment comes from emptying ourselves just like Christ and pouring life into others.

A follower of Christ is expected to put their identity in Christ. What that means is that we are expected to value others before ourselves. It's easy to focus inwardly. It's easy to focus on our own pleasure and happiness and ignore the world around us. But that goes against our design. That is not what Christ exemplifies. That is not our identity.

reflection questions

1. What are ways that people around your age pursue happiness?

2. What are activities that make you happy but that can easily distract you?

3. What experiences in your past have made you a *better* person?

4. How do we have an others-first mentality a part of our daily routine?

5. How does your life change when you view your identity in terms of helping others and not in terms of your own happiness?

"To follow Jesus is to travel sober-ly down a narrow path that is not gladly endorsed by the powers of the world."

Joe Jones

chapter five
Family / Family of God

I GREW up knowing my family was different, but I never really realized how *weird* of a family I had until I got married. Through marriage, I got an inside look at another family, and I got to see my family anew through my wife's eyes. She pointed out that my family handled conflict in a weird way (from her perspective). While her family addressed problems by never speaking about them ever, my family would descend into yelling matches since we all wanted to be right. Someone in the family would take the role of the pious mediator (usually either my brother or I), who then ended up making everything worse because they actually clearly picked a side. Then we would storm off when anger made someone do something regrettable, and then that was that. Two very different methods between our families.

I inherited some of my family's conflict strategy, and my wife inherited some of her family's conflict strategy. I talk about issues— sometimes a bit too aggressively. She does not. As you can imagine, the two styles of conflict cause conflict. It took us a bit to work everything out. This is just one example of how family sticks with us and influences us, even when we move on and start our own lives.

Our families are inescapable sources of identity. They contribute so much to what we believe and how we behave. In our pursuit of a Christ-centric, Christ-honor identity, we have to address the ways that our family and community have molded us and trained us. Whether good or bad, Christians should examine the pull of their families on their Christian witness. But when push comes to shove, we identify with the family of God over our earthly families.

family ties

Growing up, you likely think two completely opposite thoughts are true about your family: 1) They do things that most families do, and 2) My family is super weird, and no one is as strange. It's funny that we believe so many rhythms and practices and sayings and standards present in our families are just what everyone does. Yet, at the same time, we observe the embarrassing actions of our parents, the harsh rules, and the disfunction, and we sometimes think, "No other family is like that."

My family had many weird quirks—many of which I will never publish in a book. There were two primary areas as a kid where I noticed my family was different than others. One area that separated us from the masses was our choice of T.V. shows. As kids, my brother and I were not allowed to watch the highly popular show *Spongebob Squarepants*. To this day, I've maybe only seen one episode. If I remember correctly, my parents thought the show promoted "unintelligence." Another area that made my family different was that our list of cuss words included many not found on traditional lists. For instance, "crap" was banned, as was the word "stupid" for a long time. I don't think I ever said the word "stupid" until high school, besides maybe in hushed tones down dark alleys. Our choice in T.V. and in words avoided meant I very quickly noticed my family did things differently than others in the world. But when it comes to dynamics—like the conflict strategies I shared above—I didn't think we were that strange at all.

Every family is unique and different. They all have their quirks in some way, shape, or form. Unfortunately for many, some of the so-called "quirks" can be really negative. While families can lift us up, so often, they can do the worst damage when they push us down. People's experiences with family are across the board—maybe completely bad, maybe the relationship is non-existent, maybe it's super dandy, and maybe it's a mix of bad and good. Wherever you are with your family, it's important to discuss how we intentionally and unintentionally take our identities from our families.

Family allegiance is much more complicated than in Biblical times. By and large, I think the culture promotes a personal identity, so movies and media often tell us not to be defined by others. But the reality is, a lot of us are defined by our families. Our families have reputations in the community that people know, leading to expectations on us. This is especially true in rural areas, according to my wife, who hails from small-town Oklahoma. Additionally, our families invested time in us, training us either on purpose or accident how to act, and so we are a product of our upbringing. Even if we rebel against our upbringing, we are decidedly being shaped by our families—being shaped by what they are not. We have to admit that at least a part of our identity is because of our family or guardianship growing up.

Let's turn to the concept of family in the Bible. This is, of course, a major undertaking that we are going to simplify to the highlights. The Old and New Testaments reflect the values of the ancient world, where family is one of the most important associations in a person's life. In ancient times, families constituted the most basic group to which people belonged, as well as the most important and formative. Thus, a person was always primarily obligated toward familial loyalty. Kin groups came with behavioral expectations for how to treat both insiders and outsiders. Behavior and virtues like cooperation, trust, unity, and patience ideally were required in how you required in your relationship with family members.

For Israel in the Old Testament, they probably mostly interacted with those semi-closely related to them. When Abram packs up and moves from Ur to some weird place called Canaan, that would be a *major move* because it would mean (mostly) cutting family ties. God is even specific in saying to him, "Go from your country and your kindred and your father's house to the land that I will show you" (Gen. 12:1). However, he brought a lot of family with him, and when he has kids, they have to a bit of journeying to marry someone within the extended family. So much of the Old Testament is about having allegiance to your family or growing your family, or not marrying too far outside your family. There is even a commandment to "Honor your father and your mother" (Ex. 20:12)—that's one of the Top Ten non-negotiable ones. The priority of family was central to how society functioned and, in some cases, how faithful you are to God.

a different kind of "family values"

Even though respecting your family was so very important, throughout the Bible, God constantly turned family expectations upside down. In story after story in the Old Testament, younger siblings proved to be the better, grater siblings. While Christianity is thought of as a religion of "family values," Scripture shows family members who kill, enslave, have sex with, and trick one another. That's not to say these are all examples to live by; it is just to say we have plenty of examples of family values explicitly challenged. One of the most prominent ways Scripture critiques traditional family values is that God made it a habit of choosing the least important families to do the greatest things. One such example is the story of Gideon.

In the call of Gideon recorded in Judges 6, an angel comes to the man while he is hiding out from the Midianites. After Gideon questions where God is amidst all the trouble Israel is experiencing, the angel replies, in my paraphrasing: "Glad you brought that up. God is sending

YOU to take care of the Midianites and save Israel." Gideon probably gulps with fear, but he nervously replies. Judges 6:15 notes Gideon saying, "Please, Lord, how can I save Israel? Behold, my clan is the weakest in Manasseh, and I am the least in my father's house." He believes he is disqualified from being the hero because his family is worthless. Though I'm not sure how he measures the "weakness" of his clan, he is apparently from a family that doesn't amount to much. They probably don't have anyone notable in the family genealogy. They haven't really proven themselves in the public square, so they haven't earned any special honor or accolades. On top of all this, Gideon believes he is the least qualified person in his father's whole house, which he says is very, very unqualified.

But Gideon's complaints ignore that the key ingredient to success, as the angel notes in the next verse, is that God is with him. Gideon then goes on to do a lot of great things—after first testing God several times. Though he may be an unlikely hero, God empowers a person to rise out of the expectations of his family. But even after this encounter with the Angel of the Lord, family has not dropped from Gideon's mind. It's clear that through much of his story, he struggles with his identity in his family. God is pushing him to bold action, but family still lingers and defines the young judge. We see the pull toward family in one of his first missions. Judges 6:25-28 says,

> That night the Lord said to him, "Take your father's bull, and the second bull seven years old, and pull down the altar of Baal that your father has, and cut down the Asherah that is beside it and build an altar to the Lord your God on the top of the stronghold here, with stones laid in due order. Then take the second bull and offer it as a burnt offering with the wood of the Asherah that you shall cut down." So Gideon took ten

men of his servants and did as the Lord had told him.

But because he was too afraid of his family and the

men of the town to do it by day, he did it by night.

This event brings up an interesting question: Would you be comfortable telling your parents they are sinning? I have a hard enough time trying to explain an alternative interpretation of a Bible passage to my parents—I can't imagine, if they were doing some grievous sin—calling them out on it! I mean, it's hard to blame Gideon for going at night to destroy the idol. I sort of get it. That would have been a very awkward conversion at family dinner!

Of course, even by night, Gideon did do the Lord's work, so we can give him credit for that. Yet this is the second time Gideon has used his family as an excuse. At first, family was his excuse for why God should hire someone else for the gig. Now, family and community pressure are causing him to alter how he serves God. However, as the continuation of the story reveals, his dad actually defends him, saving him from death by telling them if the god Baal has a problem, then Baal can take care of the problem himself. While it ended up working out, overall, it seems to me that Gideon had his identity split between family and God.

Let's look at the New Testament. In this time period, Greeks and Romans also readily supported the idea of being loyal to family. In fact, you were expected to be closer and more loyal to your siblings over your wife—blood trumped the marriage bond! Society was structured with the family as the basic unit of the political landscape. Even if you were married, for instance, whether a guy or a girl, your father (or oldest living male relative) still had some influence over your life until he was dead. Family was such a big deal that many Romans thought that if you threatened the family, the most basic unit of society, you were threatening the function of the entire country (not unlike what many Christians believe in America). For Romans, you could threaten the family by not listening to the eldest male or by not attending to the household gods.

Family was important to life in the New Testament times. Both Jewish and Roman culture (and most of the rest of the world) respected family, albeit that played out a little differently for each culture. Just like we've already seen, it was a general rule all over the ancient world that you don't mess with family. You just don't!

And then you have Jesus changing things up.

Jesus, who some today paint as a relaxed mild-manner peacemaker possibly with a British accent, hits crowds with some real zingers about family. In no way is Jesus a revolutionary like we today sometimes think of rebels, but man, Jesus knew how to stir up crowds and flip our thinking upside down. For instance, he once casually mentions: "If anyone comes to me and does not hate his own father and mother and wife and children and brothers and sisters, yes, and even his own life, he cannot be my disciple" (Luke 14:26). Boom! Jesus just dropped a major bombshell into the life of his disciples. The context here is about counting the cost of discipleship—if you follow Jesus, you have to expect to give up everything. Even family.

This is not all Jesus says on the subject of family. Matthew's Gospel records Jesus saying the same sort of thing about the consequences of his kingdom. In Matthew 10:34-39, Jesus says:

> Do not think that I have come to bring peace to the earth. I have not come to bring peace, but a sword. For I have come to set a man against his father, and a daughter against her mother, and a daughter-in-law against her mother-in-law. And a person's enemies will be those of his own household. Whoever loves father or mother more than me is not worthy of me, and whoever loves son or daughter more than me is not

worthy of me. And whoever does not take his cross and follow me is not worthy of me. Whoever finds his life will lose it, and whoever loses his life for my sake will find it.

Welp. And Christians say we are the religion of "family values!"

It is important to understand the context of both of these passages. They are about the "cost" of following Jesus. When you join up with Jesus, here's what you should expect: families will be torn apart, tensions will rise, and things are likely to get awkward. Matthew's language better reflects the spirit of Jesus' statement about "hating" your parents in Luke. In Matthew, Jesus is clear that the issue is *loving family more than loving Jesus.*

Unchecked family loyalty can cause problems, especially to a Christian who has entered into a new kind of family (more on that in the next section). Reflecting on this passage in Matthew 10, theologian Joe Jones ponders in a sermon:

Is it not true that Jesus knows that much violence is perpetrated in the name of protecting one's family and nation from an alien enemy that is outside the family? Does Jesus correctly discern that family pride and honor are repeatedly at the root of the revenge and retaliation that literally populate the whole of human history? Perhaps Jesus is aware of a dark side to family relationships that might thwart and stand in the way of a family member becoming a disciple of Jesus?[xxii]

Scripture is filled with examples of family conflict, but so is history in general. The Hatfield–McCoy feud is one of the most legendary family feuds in American history; its length and tenancy have now become a term to describe any rivalry between parties. Mark Twain satirizes this feud in *Huckleberry Finn* when the titular character gets caught up in a long-standing feud between Grangerfords and Sheperdsons, who do not even remember why they are fighting in the first place! Family at its best can be a source of great strength, but at its worst becomes an ever-flowing fountain of violence.

Following God isn't easy. It means that we have to rethink some values of the world. Yes, how we grow up definitely affects who we are—and also we should still totally be nice to our families. However, ultimately, our priorities are not to be like them, not to please them, not to seek their approval, but our main priority is following Jesus. Jones reminds in his sermon on this theme that it is not that Jesus is creating an anti-family policy, but that Jesus is preaching that "discipleship is not simply a reinforcement of society's mores and relationships."[xxiii] Jesus is trying to get us to do relationships differently.

welcome to the family

What Jesus says about family is some of the harshest teachings that the Son of God offers us in the Gospels. But, like all that Jesus says, it is for our own good. We can get caught up in identifying with our family or in prioritizing close relations over God's call that we get distracted from the Christian mission. Luckily, in Christ, we have a clean slate whether your family was the talk of the town—for bad or good reasons—that no longer matters. Jesus's values (which should be ours, of course) are not the same as the world's values. We are not defined by our family. According to Jesus, in some cases, we are even going to have to separate drastically from our family. God has a different definition for us: we are a part of the Family of God.

In yet another instance where Jesus is a bit harsh against earthly families, Jesus shows that the new family is not based on blood but on the bond of Christ.

While he was still speaking to the people, behold, his mother and his brothers stood outside, asking to speak to him. But he replied to the man who told him, "Who is my mother, and who are my brothers?" And stretching out his hand toward his disciples, he said, "Here are my mother and my brothers! For whoever does the will of my Father in heaven is my brother and sister and mother."

Remember, family members, especially brothers and sisters, were in this time period very close. They were taught to value the needs of their siblings over their own. Taking this expectation, Jesus creates a new definition of family. In this new family, it doesn't matter if your family was rich or poor, supportive or destructive, present or absent—you are invited to experience true family. This family is based around a shared goal and shared transformation. Jesus is at the center of this family.

Becoming a Christian is being a part of a ginormous family with billions upon billions of siblings—those alive today and those that have gone before us. Even when your earthly family lets you down, doesn't understand you, or holds you back—we have this universal family to lean on and give us hope. God doesn't strip away the priority of earthly relationships and provide us nothing else; God has provided a family based on faith.

Repeatedly through the New Testament letters, you find the language of kinship for a reason. Paul especially loves to call those in the Christian family *brothers* (the Greek term can in most cases be translated gender neutrally as *brothers and sisters*). You don't have to travel far in the early church to see they constantly talked of themselves as a family, which means that the former categories no longer apply. Paul says, for instance: "in Christ Jesus you are all sons of God, through faith. For as many of you as were baptized into Christ have put on Christ. There is neither Jew nor Greek; there is neither slave nor free, there is no male and female, for you are all one in Christ Jesus" (Gal. 3:26-28). Those distinctions don't vanish in thin air, but they are meaningless when it comes to being in the Family of God.

The Family of God is not perfect since it's made up of imperfect people. But identity in the Family of God is a worthwhile identity. It is one that matters, both here on earth and the life after. In this family, we have allegiance to one and one figure only. That is not to our family, our tribe, your group, or even best friends. Above all others, our loyalty is toward our Father in Heaven.

reflection questions

1. What does the dominant culture think about family? Are they for or against it?

2. Do you wish you had a better, closer relationship with your family?

3. Does the opinion of your family shape your opinions?

4. What does it look like in your life if you have allegiance to Jesus over allegiance to your family?

5. How does your life change when you view your identity in terms of the Family of God and not in terms of your own families?

"I've never had anyone define purity. You probably can't define purity. It is to live by original design."

Josh McDowell

chapter six

Sexual Freedom / Faithful Relationships

BEFORE our marriage, my wife and I received premarital counseling through our Christian school. The school offered us fairly cheap counseling to help prep us for the big life change, and it counted toward the requirements to waive the marriage license fee. A win-win, as I see it (although when you do the math, I think we still spent more than we would have, just shucking out cash for the license without the counseling sessions). In these sessions, I am proud to report; the counselor was pleasantly surprised that we were a functional couple who had talked about many things before marriage. It might not surprise you that a lot of young Christian couples who meet in college fall in love and are hitched before you know it with very little forethought about what they were committing to.

Well, any good premarital counseling includes a discussion about sex. Ours did, though as my wife and I reflect back on it, it was talked about for like 20 minutes, and we were given pretty terrible advice. That's the subject of another book. During this awkward chat, something the counselor said stuck out to me. She said that she always automatically *assumes that the couples in her office have already been having sex*. At a conservative Christian college where members of the opposite sex were not allowed in the other dorm, where dancing was not allowed because it could "lead to things," and where PDA was passionately discouraged—still, apparently, everyone was having sex!

If sex even reached the most conservative corners of Christianity, then clearly, sexuality has a pervasive influence over our modern culture. Sexuality is a hot-button issue in our culture. An obsession with sex happens on both sides of the political divide. It is everywhere. Some people want to license-free sexual expression for everyone. Others want to control and limit sexual expression. Some people put boxes around your gender "role." Others throw off the box and place you on a spectrum. But however they work it out, it seems everyone is talking about sex.

This chapter is about identity and sexuality. It's obviously a sensitive subject, but it's an important one. It's also a complex topic. Unfortunately, there are a lot of questions about sexuality that I can't get into with a single chapter—this deserves a book, and luckily there are several resources out there, so I don't need to write one. The simple aim of his chapter is to describe the difference between a spiritually *fruitful* sexual identity and a spiritually *unfruitful* sexual identity. Our sexual identity is fruitful when it is rooted in God's plan rather than an earthly vision of sexuality. Beyond just a platitude like "save yourself for marriage," God's design for sexuality includes a focus on faithful relationships.

sexual beings being sexual

Like the first chapter where we looked at "sin," sexuality also is a muddy and confusing term. Though I started the chapter talking about *sexual intercourse*, the term *sexuality* refers to so much more. While I could turn to many places, the World Health Organization has a lengthy but comprehensive definition. For them, sexuality is:

> a central aspect of being human throughout life [which]
> encompasses sex, gender identities and roles, sexual

orientation, eroticism, pleasure, intimacy and reproduction. Sexuality is experienced and expressed in thoughts, fantasies, desires, beliefs, attitudes, values, behaviours, practices, roles and relationships. While sexuality can include all of these dimensions, not all of them are always experienced or expressed. Sexuality is influenced by the interaction of biological, psychological, social, economic, political, cultural, legal, historical, religious and spiritual factors.[xxiv]

There is a lot that goes into sexuality, and any person could mean one or more of these traits. When I refer to sexual identity, I want us to think of it in these broad terms. I like this definition because sometimes, in our culture, we only think of sexually promiscuous people as "having sex," or in some uses of language, non-heterosexuals are labeled as "sexual" while heterosexuals get a free pass for some reason. However, everyone has elements of sexuality, even if they have never been sexually active with another person. It's not just about who you sleep with. It's not just about who you are romantically interested in. It's all of this and more.

While humans are not mere creatures, we are nonetheless creaturely. Sexuality comes with the territory of having bodies. Like all creatures, we have sexual differentiation. No matter what you think about gender roles and gender expression, it is a biological reality that there are two different sexes, as encoded in DNA and as seen in genitals. Another trait we share with animals is sexual desire. Most humans want the intimacy and release of sex. And we tend to act on it, sometimes with restraint and sometimes without.

Starting at the beginning—like, pretty much the very beginning—Scripture affirms that we are sexual beings. Famously, Genesis 1:27 reveals that humans are both made in the image of God and made as "male and female." In the creation account in the next chapter, we are told that in order to keep the lonely human company, God took out the side of the person and made a female. Sexual differentiation. Curiously, this account ends with the statement that "Therefore a man shall leave his father and his mother and hold fast to his wife, and they shall become one flesh" (Gen. 2:24). While there is sexual differentiation, there is also a way to get back to a kind of previous oneness.

Sexual identity was baked into humanity from day one. Even the first command ever given to a human in the Bible is to have sex. Genesis 1:28 says, "Be fruitful and multiply and fill the earth!" We are sexual beings at our core. Thus it can be said that thinking about sex and doing sex is a part of what makes us humans. However, just because something is "natural" doesn't mean we get a free pass to do whatever we want. Eating is needed, but overeating can lead to natural bodily consequences. Similarly, how we have sex and express ourselves sexually can have consequences.

sexually controlled

Sexuality gets brought up a lot these days in the political sphere, often with the church trying to preach its values into that secular space. The central issue can often be boiled down to controlled vs. uncontrolled or boundaries vs. no boundaries, with conservatives often favoring control and liberals often favoring no boundaries. Entertainment media tends to favor the lack of boundaries side of things. It's hard to find a show where casual sex is not casually accepted. In fact, I once listened to a podcast with a Christian writer of *That's '70s Show*. While I've never seen the show, I know the premise is that a bunch of liberal teenagers are being liberal teenagers. The writer of the show revealed that the producers demanded that every bad action on the show have a consequence. So, if someone stole, the end of the episode had to have some kind of consequence or repercussion so as to protect people from thinking the show supported that behavior. But he noted that casual premarital sex (or drug use) *never* needed to have consequences. It was a behavior the studio didn't mind promoting.

Society, in general, doesn't care what happens in the bedroom. The vast majority of religiously unaffiliated people say sex between consenting adults is sometimes or always acceptable. Surprisingly, even many Christians in America have some permissive views on sex. In an August 2020 study, Pew Research notes that half of U.S. Christians say casual sex between consenting adults who are not in a romantic relationship is sometimes or always acceptable. The percentage of Christians who are sometimes or always okay with two unmarried people having sex while in a committed relationship is a bit higher-representing a *majority* of surveyed Christians.[xxv]

Based purely on the percentage of sentences in "red letters," Jesus was not as focused on sex as many modern Christians. Unfortunately, he doesn't clearly demarcate the boundaries of good and bad sex as much as we might like. Nevertheless, Jesus has some thoughts on sex. One of his main concerns is actually *sexual thoughts*. As Jesus preaches from the Mount, he calls on people to rethink sex.

> You have heard that it was said, 'You shall not commit adultery.' But I say to you that everyone who looks at a woman with lustful intent has already committed adultery with her in his heart. If your right eye causes you to sin, tear it out and throw it away. For it is better that you lose one of your members than that your whole body be thrown into hell. And if your right hand causes you to sin, cut it off and throw it away. For it is better that you lose one of your members than that your whole body go into hell.

It's the kind of statement that would wake some people up: bodily mutilation is preferred over adulterous lusting. But Jesus' strong words are a sure sign to pay attention and take the sin of lust seriously.

Lust is a hard term to define. The word just means "having a great desire." It can be used positively or negatively. Yet, a clue to its use can be found in the context. The Greek word for "lust" is also often used to translate the Hebrew word for "coveting," which is a big no-no according to the Ten Commandments (unlike lust, coveting is always viewed negatively). Coveting is usually linked to the actual act of taking, yet coveting can also have the idea of planning and specificity in regard to taking something that is not yours. Summarizing the ancient Jewish philosopher Philo, Leonard Greenspoon writes, "whereas most passions are involuntary, covetousness is under human control since it is based on an idea, namely, that something that is not yours should be yours."[xxvi]

Adding all this data together, I think we can assume that sexual lust is probably bad when the desire is a) out of control (though it is something you *could* control) or b) stirs a desire to commit the act in real life. If a dirty thought pops into your head, you are probably not sinning— especially if your first thought is to get it out. Since we are sexual beings, sometimes our brain is going to turn toward sexual thoughts. However, we do have control over our desire to act inappropriately with someone else. To put it into the real world, thinking "She's hot" is significantly different than "I want to have sex with her." Lust, then, is greater than a wandering thought.

Self-control is a major virtue for Christians, one of our fruits of the spirit. It's the foundation of so many Biblical values that link nonviolence, peacemaking, love, etc. One of my biggest complaints of liberal culture is the uncritical acceptance of any and all sexual expression. It is certainly a response to a conservative culture that is way too restrictive. Yet, the gospel demands that we examine ourselves and our expressions critically, that we make sure to keep our behaviors in check. I would love if freedom in Christ meant we could do whatever we want, but it does not. Freedom in Christ is about doing what we were designed to do. But more on that below.

Clearly, a desire for someone who is not your wife is a problem. That's been a pretty standard view since before Jesus and throughout church traditions since. But what about when you just have strong sexual desires that cannot be controlled? What happens when you got sex on the brain, and you just can't get rid of it? Paul has an answer in 1 Corinthians 7:1-9 that is a bit unconventional. He beings the chapter by affirming that sex is good in marriage and that each marriage partner has "authority" over their spouses' body. Yet, he doesn't want couples to deprive each other of sex for too long. He even relates the issues back to self-control: "come together again, so that Satan may not tempt you because of your lack of self-control" (1 Cor. 7:5).

But then Paul gets into his real thoughts on marriage. He writes:

> Now as a concession, not a command, I say this. I wish
> that all were as I myself am. But each has his own gift
> from God, one of one kind and one of another. To the
> unmarried and the widows I say that it is good for them
> to remain single, as I am. But if they cannot exercise
> self-control, they should marry. For it is better to marry
> than to burn with passion. (1 Cor. 7:6-9).

Paul affirms sex is good—within a marriage. There are a couple of reasons for this. Here, his reasoning seems to be about *self-control*. Marriage is a "controlled" and "allowable" setting. It's the proper place for sexual desires. Desires are not bad, but there is a time and a place. As a married person, however, this whole conversation makes me feel like Paul is saying that the purpose of marriage is just sex. We've all probably heard wedding sermons that talk about how God created the institution of marriage and that it's founded in love—1 Corinthians 13 was probably quoted at least once. Yet in chapter 7, Paul seems to be saying that you get married if you are *super horny and need the release*. That's not a marriage sermon I've ever heard. That's not a marriage sermon I'd ever *want* to hear.

With singleness, Paul seems to say that a true display of self-control is to not be controlled by sexual desires. As already mentioned, self-control of your desires is a big part of Christianity. We recognize that our natural urges are not always great, and Jesus demonstrated to us how to put aside natural urges (hunger and sex) to focus on spiritual matters. However, not everyone is cut out for celibacy, as even Paul himself affirms. Best we can, great lust is something Christians must try to control.

uniting with others

The cure for an overreliance on our own sexuality—including our sexual thoughts, sexual activities, and sexual identity—is to remember who we are in relation to others. We do not live in our "own little world," but in a world where everyone is intricately connected. Instead of making sexual unions and sexual satisfaction a hallmark of our identities, Christians are better served when we construct our identity in terms of loving relationships with other people. This, in turn, affects how we conceive of our own sexuality.

Since Jesus was a human, he had a lot of the same desires we do. Although he was celibate his whole life, he wasn't void of sexuality. One of my theology professors once said Jesus probably got an accidental erection from time to time. The thought has haunted me since. Yet maybe it is helpful for us to remember that Jesus experiences desires like us. The key difference, though, is that he never acted on those desires.

He maintained control over his body and desires and did not let them lead to improper behavior.

Sexuality might make us human, but self-control makes us more than merely natural creatures. Jesus, the "single savior," enacts God's design of controlled sexuality. This view of sexuality has been the divine plan since the beginning. As scholar R.R. Reno says about sexuality in Genesis:

> Without doubt, human sexuality is instinctual, just as our cognitive faculties are part of the natural equipment of our bodily existence. But instincts and natural abilities must be educated and shaped so that they take a specific form in an actual human life. From the beginning, the divine plan was and remains the same: to order our natural capacities toward our supernatural vocation.[xxvii]

A principal issue with some modern notions of bodily autonomy—like the phrase "my body, my choice" (which can be applied to many cases besides abortion)—is that, for the Christian, our body actually doesn't belong to us. Paul is trying to make this point in 1 Corinthians 6 when the congregation there is just really not understanding sex. He begins in 1 Corinthians 6:12-13 by modifying some quotes he likely heard from the Corinthians.

> 'All things are lawful for me,' but not all things are helpful. 'All things are lawful for me,' but I will not be dominated by anything. 'Food is meant for the stomach and the stomach for food'—and God will destroy both one and the other. The body is not meant for sexual immorality, but for the Lord, and the Lord for the body.

Our true ownership of our bodies and of our sexuality is in the Lord. This has lots of ramifications, as Paul goes on to explain in verses 15-20

> Do you not know that your bodies are members of Christ? Shall I then take the members of Christ and

make them members of a prostitute? Never! Or do you not know that he who is joined to a prostitute becomes one body with her? For, as it is written, "The two will become one flesh." But he who is joined to the Lord becomes one spirit with him. Flee from sexual immorality. Every other sin a person commits is outside the body, but the sexually immoral person sins against his own body. Or do you not know that your body is a temple of the Holy Spirit within you, whom you have from God? You are not your own, for you were bought with a price. So glorify God in your body.

We are humans with human desires—but as believers—we are under new management. We are holy temples, and temples cannot be defiled by giving in to the lusts of our flesh. Instead, we are to be people of self-control. Elsewhere, Paul declares that it is the will of God that a person should "know how to control his own body in holiness and honor, not in the passion of lust like the Gentiles who do not know God" (1 Thess. 4:4-5). We are to glorify God with how we act sexually.

While this feels like restriction, not freedom, it actually is freedom. True freedom releases us from all the bondages we take for granted. Christ has set us free from the bondage of sin and the slavery of the law (Gal. 5:1). If sin is the powers of the world that control us, then with Christ, we are freed from serving those powers (though not free from being influenced by them). We submit to Christ because through him, and we can have an abundance of life. Now that we are free from controlling elements and aimed toward Christ, we can use that freedom constructively—what some theologians call *freedom for*. Perhaps the best way to combat an overreliance on sexual freedom is to replace it with a deep love for others. I love how Martin Luther frames Christian liberty: "A Christian man is the freest lord of all, and subject to none; a Christian man is the most dutiful servant of all, and subject to everyone."[xxviii] This is not a mere contradiction but explains the weird place that Christians inhabit in the world. Luther gleans both statements from Paul, mainly Romans 14:8 and 1 Corinthians 9:19, which speak of our obligation to others. We find a new identity and new freedom when we cast off an overfocus on sexuality and put a focus on building relationships with others.

In most cases, sexuality revolves around other people. In Scripture's first account, where sexuality comes into play, it's about other people. As people made in the image of God, we have the ability to bring life into the world—though not quite *ex nihilo*. One significant way heterosexual sexual intercourse can affect other people is because it can *create another person*. The fact that sexual intercourse can bring to the world life makes it, in some ways, dangerous because of the value of life and the Christian responsibility to care for the life we produce (as God cares for us). Yet this does not mean that every Christian is tasked with producing the future. Genesis 1:28's insistence on being "fruitful and multiple" should not be taken *only* as a reference to getting busy with baby-making. People are given dominion over the earth and are *supposed to do something with it*. We are fruitful in way more ways than just our ability to create life.

Then in Genesis 2, we find a description of creation that stresses that humankind was created with a desire for fellowship. Reno notes that while Genesis 1 was about "cosmic" purpose, the next chapter deals with more personal fulfillment.[xxix] While it may be tempting to make Genesis 2 about marriage, we need not put those labels on it. There isn't even anything explicitly "romantic" about the encounter. It's true, Adam is drawn to Eve, and the result is procreation, and there is a prediction about a time when people will leave their parents to be united to another. The deeper theme is actually longing and community. Genesis 2:5-7 affirms that God created man because the earth had no one to work it.

So then the first man was formed from the ground. Likewise, the man had no companion—literally, no "helper." So the first woman was formed from the original person. Eve, the mother of all living, didn't appear because Adam was *horny* but because he needed help. God says, "It is not good that the man should be alone." While they do end up having a sexual relation (later tainted by sin, which brings shame to their sexuality), their relationship is first formed on the foundation of desire and mutual assistance. It models all relationships—not just marital ones.

Our relationship with people is vastly more important than our individual sexual expression. God doesn't put down rules about sex just because God is a cosmic killjoy, but because *improper sexual behavior hurts and affects people*. In 1 Thessalonians 4:6, in the context of Paul reminding the Thessalonians of the Christian sexual ethic, he urges "that no one transgress and wrong his brother [or sister] in this matter." While he is specifically talking about a church context (since the church is a family), we can see that one person's sexual ethics affect others. Not controlling one's body results in the violation of the command to love one's neighbor. I like how one scholar, Robert Yarbrough puts it: "Paul does not want his readers to practice sex like the heathens do because he does not want to see the error of πορνεία (immorality) mushroom to the scandal of πλεονεκτεῖν (depriving others of God-given status and dignity), which is clearly transgression (ὑπερβαίνειν)."[xxx] In many cases today, we can practice sex in ways that are degrading and undignified—even if the act is consensual. For instance, sex can be weaponized in a relationship to get one partner to do what you want, guilt or shame can be used to evoke sexual activity, or adultery can dishonor the person you sleep with and the person's spouse. All of these are ways in which sex can exploit and dehumanize people.

Thus, more important than our own sexual urges is how we control those urges in service to others. Our greater calling is to a healthy relationship. This includes but is not limited to marriage. We must seek connections with others, especially those in the Christian community, to fulfill our deepest longing for others. We are incomplete without community. It was not good for man to be alone, and it still is not. There is a part of our identity that is found in our healthy relationships with others; we are not whole all alone.

Desires are not bad, but actually acting on them can be bad, depending on the nature of the desires. Sometimes we are going to eat when we are hungry—and a lot of us will probably end up having sex sometime because it feels good. As Christians, we are called to go beyond primal, natural desires and instead be driven by the Spirit in healthy mutual relationships. Our identity is not in sexual desires—that's not who we really are. We are so much more. Our identity is in our healthy relationships with others.

reflection questions

1. In your own terms, what is "healthy sexuality" and what is "unhealthy sexuality?"
2. What does it look like to "control your own body?"
3. How can we balance completely natural sexual urges and preferences with more important values?
4. What does it look like to nurture healthy, Christ-centered relationships?
5. How would your life change if you view your identity in terms of creating healthy relationships with others and not in terms of your sexuality?

"Like all men who are fundamentally of the group, of the herd, he was incapable of taking a strong stand with the inevitable loneliness that it implied."

F. Scott Fitzgerald

chapter seven
Groups / Kingdom of God

FOR as long as I have been alive, every four years when a Presidential election comes around, tensions rise in the nation, and individual people adopt the façade of their preferred political parties. They start spouting the same talking points as their team. They use the same rhetoric. They demonize the other side and anyone else they want to blame for the nation's problems. Things get nasty. People I once recognized as decent people become anything but decent people.

But politics are not the only thing that gets people to throw off all sense and sensitivity to protect what they hold dear. Lots of groups that people align themselves with can quickly eat up individuality and blind you to some of the realities of the complex world. This chapter is meant to push back against the group identities that we adopt and hold dear, especially our allegiance to political parties and similar associations. Any number of false identities could have appeared as the seventh and final. Yet so much hate and objectively unchristian behavior come from the earthly groups and movements we uncritically join. Some of these groups are not inherently bad—there is no reason to throw them out completely—but we have to realize when the groups are shaping us.

grouping up

There are generally three categories of people when it comes to group projects at school. You have the perfectionist annoyed by the inadequacies of the group members, you have the worker bees that wait for orders and do what they are told, and finally, you have the slacker who loves group projects because it means they can make others do the work. For most of my school years, I fell into the first category of people. Group projects were the bane of my existence, threatening my excellent grades, my high standards, and my general intolerance for slackers. I didn't even like team sports for fear that I would let down others and that they would let me down. There are lots like me that want to do their own thing, but even the highly individualists often find comfort and solidarity as a part of a group, a fandom, an association, a tribe. People like to belong.

As we discussed in the previous chapter, humankind is not made to be alone. There is something powerful about association with one another. As the Preacher so eloquently puts it,

> Two are better than one, because they have a good reward for their toil. For if they fall, one will lift up his fellow. But woe to him who is alone when he falls and has not another to lift him up! Again, if two lie together, they keep warm, but how can one keep warm alone? [12] And though a man might prevail against one who is alone, two will withstand him—a threefold cord is not quickly broken. (Ecc. 4:9-12).

Companionship, friends, groups—they are all important. Jesus founds the church as a cord that cannot be broken as it is empowered by the Holy Spirit and strengthened by our bond with each other. In an ideal world, groups would only bring strength to help regular fellows do some really awesome things.

It helps to under a bit of the psychology behind why groups are so important. As the article "Why People Join Fanatical Groups" in *Psychology Today* explains, people often join groups—even fanatical groups—for a sense of belonging. In the article, the authors explain:

As humans, we seem to have a built-in expectation that we will fit somewhere, that people will acknowledge us and care about us, that, in short, we will be in a band. When we don't fit, when we don't get acknowledged, we lose our bearings. Many people still get their fundamental identity from family, but families can sometimes be poisonous environments where anxious, neglectful, or violent parents pass their psychological problems on to their children. So people join gangs, clubs, churches, and teams and pledge their allegiance to nations and to corporations.[xxxi]

We intricately want to attach ourselves to something. We have some spare allegiance to give out to someone or something; we just need to pick someone or something. And once you join that group, it begins to influence our lives. You are adopted into that culture to speak their language, read their resources, and believe what they want you to believe. A group can become a convenient source for your identity.

Through this entire book, we have been working our way through identities that we give too much power, those identities where we uncritically pledge our loyalty. So far, with the exception of chapter five on family, the focus has been on internal values—standards we put on ourselves to live and die by. This last chapter reminds us that problems with identity formation are not just found in our personalities or individual behaviors but are in the groups we join up with. Whatever group we choose to go all-in for—whether that be the Christian community or something else—that association is going to change us. So we must choose wisely.

Admittedly, politics is the easy target in all this. But that's because it's one of the most common allegiances people have, and it has great effects on how we behave. As Kaitlyn Schiess argues in *The Liturgy of Politics*, building off the work of James K.A. Smith in *Awaiting the King*, politics forms us and shapes our nature through rituals and effective language. There is a great sense in which the ideas and behaviors associated with our political associations tell us who to love and how to love. Schiess explains that shaping people is the whole goal of politics when she writes, "Political projects have a teleology—they are moving in the direction of a certain view of what the world should be like, how humans should act, and good goals we should be working toward."[xxxii] So when we decide to join a particular political party or watch a particular source of political news, or pledge allegiance to a particular nation and its political system, then we must be aware of the power that the group can have over us.

Because of the power of groups, groups can become dangerous. Groupthink has wrecked loads of damage throughout history. Christian history is specifically ripe with examples where a large majority of people thought a *bad idea was actually good*—any number of popular heresies, wars, inquisitions, crusades, slave trades, etc. In some of these cases, the danger came from uncritically aligning ourselves to the Christian Faith, but in other cases, it is an uncritical allegiance to other groups, like the nation, a political party, or even a particular race. I mean, even guys like Hitler had the backing of many people of faith. We must remain diligent that we don't repeat the mistakes of the past and sign over our allegiance to a group that does not deserve our unwavering support.

Perhaps another explanation for both the pull toward groups and the power groups have over us is that we humans don't like complexity. We want to take shortcuts if we can. So if our favorite media outlet says something is true, we accept it and will fight others to confirm the statement of the media outlet. The world becomes organized into the categories "us" and "them." It's my group vs. everyone else. Schiess explains, "We use our categories when we want to quickly evaluate the value of a media source (Are they on my team?), a commentator (Is he or she one of us?), or the personality at the center of a story (Is he or she like me?)."[xxxiii] The issue with this reasoning—though it's so common—is that it gets us in trouble too easily. We no longer have to think critically but have outsourced the process to other people. And the only credentials these others might have is that they are in your group; they agree with your presuppositions already.

There are several other reasons we may join up with a group. Many of us Christians would claim that our faith is the primary motivator to enter the fight for a particular cause or team up with a group (I wish that were so, but so often that's not the case). We join groups for an identity, for a way to fit into the social strata of an environment (think *Mean Girls* or really any movie about high school). We join groups for security (to have protection against those we perceive as enemies and to avoid). We join groups to have social connections (especially important in an increasingly isolated world). Similarly, we join groups to bond over a shared activity (fandoms, sports clubs, and the like). Whatever the reasons, we must take a cold, hard look at any time we join a group with the power to shape our identity.

where allegiances lie

Allow me to summarize the Hebrew Scriptures from Exodus onward: *The Israelites are attracted to what another group is doing, and they abandon God. God finally brings them back, but they abandon God all over again.* Israel's story is the story of a kid at a candy store. Constantly, they are distracted by interesting things around them. In the candy store of the world stage, it's almost impossible to get them to focus for a second on the true task at hand. The world is constantly pulling at God's people, demanding they make a choice of allegiance.

In the Old Testament, the pull is often around idols. In modern preaching, we tend to think of idols as "something we really like" or "something that distracts us from God." Those aren't wrong, but they aren't the whole story. Today we might say staying up late on a Saturday night to play video games makes an "idol" out of video games because it might make you miss the church the next morning. But Israel's problem wasn't just that idols and false gods were really cool or distracting to worship of Yahweh. The problem ran much deeper.

The central issue is that idols represented a form of security. Baal, one of the more popular foreign gods we find in the Old Testament, is the god of fertility. He both assured that crops were fertile and abundant and that animals and people were fertile and abundant. If an Israelite was really worried about having a good year of crops or wanted some kids, they might hedge their bets and sacrifice to Baal. They would team up with a foreign religion for the safety, security, and the added bonus of belonging with the people in the land. One reason Israelites were forbidden from marrying foreigners was to curb the appeal of alternative systems. God didn't want Israel to team up with anything or anyone else besides Yahweh. The voice of the Lord is clear in Jeremiah 10:2-3, "Learn not the way of the nations, nor be dismayed at the signs of the heavens because the nations are dismayed at them, for the customs of the peoples are vanity." In other words, don't align yourself with the other nations since their values are not God's values.

According to 1 Samuel 8, Israel pleaded for a king because the other nations were doing it. The elders of Israel came to Samuel and said, "Behold, you are old and your sons do not walk in your ways. Now appoint for us a king to judge us like all the nations" (8:5). When Samuel tries to talk some sense into them, they just shrug their shoulders. 1 Samuel 8:19-20 tells us the people's response, "But the people refused to obey the voice of Samuel. And they said, 'No! But there shall be a king over us, that we also may be like all the nations, and that our king may judge us and go out before us and fight our battles.'" God consented to the whole project, but can't you just imagine God sarcastically saying something like, "If all your friends were jumping off a bridge, would you?" Why God said yes, we might never fully know. But it's clear that the Israelites were willing to give up a lot in order to look like others. They drifted from God's unique design for the nation and instead conformed to the image of the nation of the world—the biggest group there is.

The pull of groups is even more evident in the New Testament. Paul's letters in the New Testament show that early Christians had some trouble remaining distinct from the groups around them. A good example is found in 1 Corinthians. One of the chief aims of the correspondence is to reorient the Corinthians toward Christ-centered values since they have apparently strayed away.[xxxiv] It is quite possible the Christians in Corinth saw their Christian identity as "inferior" to the Roman world, so they adopted the strategy of changing their values to match the values of the "superior" group. It appears the Corinthians loved Greek philosophy and rhetoric—worldly wisdom—and so put those standards on others. Thus, Paul has to remind them that the world thinks the Christian project is foolish. True wisdom only comes from God. To access that wisdom, we must have the Spirit of God, which is not something we can get from any outside sources (1 Cor. 2:12-13).

They also struggle with groups centered around people, like Paul himself, Apollos, or Cephas (Peter). So in 3:3-4, Paul asks the rhetorical questions, "For while there is jealousy and strife among you, are you not of the flesh and behaving only in a human way? For when one says, 'I follow Paul,' and another, 'I follow Apollos,' are you not being merely human?" By being "human," they have aligned themselves with values that are not of the Spirit. They have joined themselves with people and groups. At the end of chapter 3, Paul then declares:

> Let no one deceive himself. If anyone among you thinks that he is wise in this age, let him become a fool that he may become wise. For the wisdom of this world is folly with God. For it is written, "He catches the wise in their craftiness," and again, "The Lord knows the thoughts of the wise, that they are futile." So let no one

boast in men. For all things are yours, whether Paul or Apollos or Cephas or the world or life or death or the present or the future—all are yours, and you are Christ's, and Christ is God's.

In other words, the world isn't actually offering us anything of value. It's not bad to listen to the teachings of Apollos or something, but our primary identity is in Christ. The Christian community is the group to which we primarily belong.

At the end of the day, we have to ask where our allegiance lies. In Joshua's words, "choose this day whom you will serve" (Josh. 24:15). It is not enough to just *say* that our primary allegiance is to the Kingdom of God. We must dig deep into our soul and find when we are idolizing another group or person, or when we are going along with the flow of others to fit in, or when we import the standards of the world into the church, or when we uncritically get behind a certain leader. Our allegiance is to God and God alone. Earthly groups must never come before God and us.

the transcendent kingdom

I don't know all the groups in your life that have received your pledge of loyalty. So I can't tell you which must go and which must stay. Be cautious, however, when patriotism turns into nationalism, when appreciation for a group grows into a righteous exclusivity, or when a group's unique perspective becomes the *only* perspective you listen to. Groups become dangerous when you primarily listen to them for advice on how to think, who to love, who to hate, and how to live. At that point, some otherworldly group has taken over the role of God. Your knitting club or Trekkie Facebook group probably aren't in that dangerous category—but be diligent so that groups don't override your identity in God's transcendent Kingdom.

To pledge loyalty to God and to God alone does not preclude these other identities. But it does reprioritize and transform them. Schiess writes that "Our national identities, racial or ethnic communities, and our smaller local affiliations all demand a certain kind of loyalty from us. Yet those loyalties are only rightly placed when they find their context and meaning in light of the ultimate loyalty we have to the body of Christ."[xxxv] Our identity in Christ should transcend all other identities. We must move from identifying with powerful groups into identifying with the powerful Kingdom of God.

Simply put, the Kingdom of God refers to the reign of God over all things. While creation exists only because of God's continuous blessing and God indeed can control everything, there is still a sense in which creation is in rebellion against God's rule. The presence of sin and disobedience means that the world is not yet fully a part of God's kingdom. The Kingdom of God is what Israel was supposed to be but could never be until Jesus stepped onto the scene—a nation run by God alone as a light to the world. But unlike the expectations of many Jews during Jesus' time, this kingdom is not an earthly dominion. Joe Jones describes the kingdom as "a radically new form of social reality, of social relations, of political relations. … As such a new social reality, the kingdom of God stands in contrast to the social worlds in which humans now live—in contrast to worldly, human kingdoms and their modes of rule and political power."[xxxvi] This kingdom is incomparable to anything we have on earth, as it is the complete fulfillment of the Gospel, unmarred by sin.

As is common to say about the Kingdom of God, the Kingdom is both "now" and "not yet." The Kingdom has broken into our existence with Jesus entering the world. Even before the crucifixion, Jesus was saying, "The time is fulfilled, and the kingdom of God is at hand; repent and believe in the gospel" (Mk. 1:15)—a statement which the verse before identifies as the very gospel of God. The "gospel" is the good news. The language is drawn from a Greek word that referred to the announcement of a new king. Believing in the gospel thus has a lot to do with recognizing that God is the one on the throne. But, of course, not everything is under the reign of God yet. One day, every knee shall bow before God (Rom. 14:11; Phil. 2:9-11). We now wait for that day with eagerness and longing.

Though the kingdom's completion happens later, we participate in the kingdom in the here and now. The church is not synonymous with the kingdom but is a part of the kingdom. Jones writes, "the church is called to be that new social reality that is the presence of the kingdom in human history."[xxxvii] The church is the Kingdom of God realized on earth in real-time, an outpost, an embassy for the coming kingdom. The kingdom does not need human hands to break into the world, but the church does do the work of preparing the world for this new reality. As a church, we pray, "Your kingdom come, your will be done, on earth as it is in heaven" (Matt. 6:10), and we try to make the church like that kingdom best we can, as is God's will on earth.

All this talk about the Kingdom of God may seem like I've gotten off track from the point of this passage. Trust me; it's all important. Once we have thrown off our allegiances to human-made groups—whether that be special interest groups, political parties, or event the influence of the cool kids on the block—that allegiance needs to go somewhere. This book has already shown that our loyalty cannot be placed inwardly, nor in our achievements, nor in our family. As we cast off loyalty to these groups, we must therefore pledge undying allegiance to the Kingdom of God. We must place God as the King of our lives. We must invite Christ's transformation of our character. We must latch on to the wisdom of the Spirit over the wisdom of the world. It is the gospel that should shape the norms of our lives, not the patterns of other people.

The way believers in Christ wage war has often reflected allegiance to the wrong kingdom. For 2,000 years since Christ, Christians have unfortunately found themselves in arms to protect earthly kingdoms, which they mistook for God's Kingdom. Moreover, history has recorded plenty of times where Christians battle against *each other*. Extreme group identification is often to blame—like identification with a country, a denomination, or a political movement. The American Civil War is a chilling example. During this time, the Baptists, Presbyterians, and Methodists all divided over issues of slavery, politics, and the interpretation of Scripture. While I don't want to downplay the significant moral depravity of slavery, we shouldn't forget that much of that war was about government policy. Christians of the same nation, tongue, and tradition hitched themselves to either side and killed their brothers and sisters in the faith over allegiance to earthly power.

The Kingdom of God transcends ethnic, national, political, social, geographical, and cultural barriers. Certain groups *might* display Christian values better than other groups, but we cannot say that those groups are synonymous with being a Christian. Our Christian identity is found in the Kingdom; those groups that seem acceptable to us have merely stumbled upon Christian virtues, but they themselves are not to be equated with the Kingdom. The Kingdom of God stands above and often against the groups we form in this world. It changes everything.

The Kingdom of God does not demand *disengagement* from the world but a *witness* to the world. We still "seek the welfare of the city" (Jer. 29:7) even though the Kingdom does not have its origin in this world (John 18:36). We testify not just the fact of God's reign but the character of God's reign. As Jesus pronounces time and time against in the gospels, entering this kingdom requires emptying oneself, humility, selflessness, suffering, and a concern for the marginalized. As we live out this character, we will by necessity be engaged with the world in righting wrongs, bringing peace, and challenging the normal categories that the world puts people in. Any group we join for belonging, security, social approval, or power pales in comparison to the mighty kingdom of God, where one inexplicably enters like a lowly insignificant child (Matt. 18:3-4; Mk. 10:15).

You can love your nation.

You can love your close friends.

You can love your team.

You can love your church tradition or denomination.

You can love your political party.

But all of those must submit to the authority of God in your life. They must not distract you or tear you from being a true witness to the kingdom. To form an identity in Christ, to adopt Christ's vision for your life, is to treat those groups as potentially expendable, anchoring your allegiance fully on Christ and nothing else. You either put your identity in Christ or in the world—but you cannot do both.

reflection questions

1. What groups do you enjoy being a part of? Why do you think that is?

2. Why do you think people get so worked up over politics?

3. Has there been a time where the values or actions of peers went against your Christian convictions? How did that play out?

4. What does it look like demonstrated loyalty and allegiance to the Kingdom of God in your day-to-day life?

5. How would your life change if you view your identity in terms of your allegiance to the Kingdom and not in terms of groups?

conclusion

THE twenty-somethings is a time of change, transition, and decisions. Not just one change, but many. Not just one transition, but many. Not just one decision, but many. So much that a twentysomething does and chooses will set her on a path for the rest of her life. It's all very daunting. It's a prime time to figure out the answer to the question "who am I?"

I am just a twentysomething myself. I haven't fully figured out who I am, at least in a worldly sense. Week to week, I change what I want to do as a career. My ideals for a family constantly evolve—then shift back, then change again. Hobbies and interests come and go. I'm still working out who I want to become, in a personal sense. I did not write this book thinking I am an expert on "finding yourself" or even in the Christian faith—I wrote it as a fellow traveler in this weird time of life. While I have hardly any clue what I'll be up to in five years, there are some things I am certain about. I am certain that my primary identity must be in Christ.

We worship a Savior who conquered death and is bringing the world under the full reign of God where sin and all the undesirable in life are destroyed. This Savior offers us a role and inheritance in this reign. Christ dwells in us and we in Christ—a beautiful but complicated divine embrace. We don't identify with Christ to earn Heaven, nor to get material benefits, nor even to be happier. But this new identity fulfills the deepest longings in us that nothing else can fulfill. We find that identity in Christ isn't always what we want, but it is what we need.

Jesus comes to earth as the fullest revelation of God. Our best source for God is Jesus Christ. One of the core things Jesus reveals is that

God's values are so, so, so different than our own. We've been playing the game by the wrong rules, in fact. God offers us a better way to live. God, through Jesus Christ, offers us a better identity.

> We know our intrinsically sinful, messed up state—but God gives grace.

> We long for success and the security it brings—but God offers us a new heart.

> We are haunted by the past—but God promises a better future.

> We get sucked into wanting happiness—but God shows us fulfillment in helping others.

> We are burdened and defined by family—but God presents a new family for us.

> We are compelled by sexual desires—but God blesses us with intimate relationships.

> We are caught up in persuasive groups—but God reigns over a greater Kingdom.

Casting off previous identities that cannot satisfy us, we embrace our identity in Christ in the various ways that God desires for us to live our lives. We no longer ask "who am I?" as if we are alone in this project, but we embrace our new identity as a community bonded with Christ. The church, as the witness in the world to the great Kingdom of God, comes alongside us in this transformative project. Together, we loudly declare to the world what Christ has done for us and how that radically changes *who we are*.

"It is no longer I who live, but Christ who lives in me."
Galatians 2:20

notes

The Starting Point
[i] Jones, *The Grammar of Christian Faith*, v1. 336.

[ii] Scot McKnight coins this term in *Pastor Paul*. Scot McKnight, *Pastor Paul*, 4.

[iii] This summarizes Macaskill's thesis of his whole book. Macaskill, *Living in Union with Christ*, 1 [emphasis in original].

[iv] Gorman, *The Apostle of the Crucified Lord*, 140-1, 146.

[v] https://www.oikoumene.org/en/resources/documents/assembly/2006-porto-alegre/2-plenary-presentations/christian-identity-religious-plurality/rowan-williams-presentation

[vi] Beverly Roberts Gaventa, "The Cosmic Power of Sin in Paul's Letter to the Romans: Toward a Widescreen Edition," *Interpretation* 58, no. 3 (July 2004), 235.

Chapter One: Sin / God's Grace
[vii] Anderson, *Sin: A History*, 13.

[viii] D.A. Carson, "Sin's Contemporary Significance" in *Fallen: A Theology of Sin*, pg. 28.

[ix] Cortex, *Theological Anthropology*, 40.

[x] Alcorn, *The Purity Principal*, 12.

[xi] deSilva, *Honor, Patronage, Kinship & Purity*, 129.

[xii] deSilva, *Transformation*, 11.

Chapter Two: Success / Heart for God
[xiii] https://www.imdb.com/title/tt4399942/characters/nm0000120

[xiv] Paul Tillich, *Dynamics of Faith*, Reprint (New York: Perennial Classics, 2001), 4.

[xv] Stanley Hauerwas, *Matthew* (Grand Rapids, MI: Brazos Press, 2006), 78.

Chapter Three: Past / Future Promise
[xvi] Phyllis A. Bird, "The Harlot as Heroine: Narrative Art and Social Presupposition in Three Old Testament Texts," *Semeia* 46 (1989), 120.

[xvii] Judith Baskin, "The Rabbinic Transformations of Rahab the Harlot," *Notre Dame English Journal* 11, no. 2 (1979), 144.

[xviii] https://jwa.org/encyclopedia/article/rahab-bible

Chapter Four: Happiness / Helping Others

[xix] C.S. Lewis, *Mere Christianity*, 129.

[xx] Lewis, *Mere Christianity*, 131.

[xxi] Thomas. *The Imitation of Christ*. Grand Rapids, Mich: Generic NL Freebook Publisher. Accessed August 28, 2020. Chapter 15.

Chapter Five: Success / Heart for God

[xxii] Jones, Joe R.. A Lover's Quarrel: A Theologian and His Beloved Church (p. 177). Cascade Book - An Imprint of Wipf and Stock Publishers.

[xxiii] Jones, Joe R.. A Lover's Quarrel: A Theologian and His Beloved Church (p. 179). Cascade Book - An Imprint of Wipf and Stock Publishers.

Chapter Six: Sexual Freedom / Faithful Relationships

[xxiv] (https://www.who.int/reproductivehealth/topics/sexual_health/sh_definitions/en/, accessed 09/30/2019)

[xxv] https://www.pewresearch.org/fact-tank/2020/08/31/half-of-u-s-christians-say-casual-sex-between-consenting-adults-is-sometimes-or-always-acceptable/

[xxvi] https://www.thetorah.com/article/do-not-covet-is-it-a-feeling-or-an-action

[xxvii] Reno, *Genesis*, 75.

[xxviii] https://sourcebooks.fordham.edu/mod/luther-freedomchristian.asp

[xxix] Reno, *Genesis*, 75.

[xxx] Yarbrough, "Sexual Gratification in 1 Thess. 4:1-8," 226.

Chapter Seven: Groups / Kingdom of God

[xxxi] https://www.psychologytoday.com/us/blog/evolution-in-daily-life/201911/why-people-join-fanatical-groups

[xxxii] Schiess, Kaitlyn. The Liturgy of Politics, pp. 24. InterVarsity Press.

[xxxiii] Schiess, Kaitlyn. The Liturgy of Politics (p. 30). InterVarsity Press. Kindle Edition.

[xxxiv] Tucker, *You Belong to the Lord*, 35.

[xxxv] Schiess, Kaitlyn. The Liturgy of Politics (p. 30). InterVarsity Press. Kindle Edition.

[xxxvi] Jones, *The Grammar of Christian Faith*, 701.

[xxxvii] Jones, *The Grammar of Christian Faith*, 703.

CPSIA information can be obtained
at www.ICGtesting.com
Printed in the USA
BVHW040117280421
605957BV00008B/1976